"Marilyn Loden's work—*Implementing Diversity*—is a milestone in the integration of diversity initiatives in the field of organization change. She provides a critical analysis of the need for organizations to do diversity work provided they desire success in the 21st century. Her case studies, diagnostic instruments, and cautions to HR professionals, OD consultants and executives creates the most comprehensive guide to date on planning an organization's growth with a diverse workforce. The millennium's rapid approach—and the present climate of change—means that we can't ignore diversity. And the added value that it brings to organizations means that *Implementing Diversity* is simply required reading for anybody involved in an organizational change effort."

Lennox Joseph, Ph.D.
President and Chief Executive Officer
NTL Institute

"*Implementing Diversity* is great exercise for both sides of the brain—it offers interesting conceptual approaches, understanding of human behavior as well as experienced pragmatism and logical steps for building a plan. As a concept, the approach to diversity which Marilyn Loden characterizes as "Diversity Includes Everyone" is valuable in communicating to a broad audience and includes a natural and comfortable focus on core diversity issues such as gender and race. *Implementing Diversity* offers understanding about human and organizational behavior and some practical steps to attaining a better workplace for all."

Dan C. Stanzione
President
AT&T Bell Laboratories

"In this era of ever-expanding world markets and opportunities, Marilyn Loden has produced yet another sensible and far-sighted guide for making the American work place exciting, fulfilling and productive for all workers. A job training and management specialist, she has written extensively on how to build effective teamwork, and her latest book, *Implementing Diversity,* outlines specific strategies for encouraging commitment and excellence from the whole human family with all its many differences in ethnicity, religion and sexual orientation."

Diane Feinstein
United States Senator

"Filled with new ideas and practical insights. A must read for managers and diversity specialists."

J. Randall MacDonald
Senior Vice President—Human Resources
GTE Corporation

Implementing Diversity

IMPLEMENTING DIVERSITY

DIVERSITY

Marilyn Loden

- Dozens of Practical Tips for Leading the Change Effort

- 12 Classic Mistakes Most Organizations Make and How to Avoid Them

Boston, Massachusetts   Burr Ridge, Illinois
Dubuque, Iowa   Madison, Wisconsin   New York, New York
San Francisco, California   St. Louis, Missouri

McGraw-Hill

A Division of The McGraw·Hill Companies

© Marilyn Loden, 1996.

Library of Congress Cataloging-in-Publication Data

Loden, Marilyn.
   Implementing diversity / Marilyn Loden.
      p.   cm.
   Includes index.
   ISBN 0–7863–0460–X
    1. Diversity in the workplace—United States. I. Title.
HF5549.5.M5L63 1995
658.3'041—dc20   95–20775
                                                   CIP

Printed in the United States of America

8 9 BKM BKM   0 9 8 7 6 5 4 3 2

For my mother: Mary C. Downey

with special thanks to John Loden
and Reg Bowes.

PREFACE

Ten years ago when I wrote *Feminine Leadership* (my first book about diversity), I pointed out some of the ways in which gender differences impact leadership styles. In exploring gender differences, I wanted to underscore the value that could be added to organizational decision making, teamwork, and innovation when greater style diversity was encouraged. In that early book, I chose what I thought were obvious examples of the ways in which women's skills were often underutilized. At the time, I did not anticipate that pointing out those differences would provoke the kind of spirited discussion and even controversy that have occurred since.

Similarly, despite more than 20 years of change management consulting in Fortune 500 companies, universities, public agencies, and law and consulting firms, I was not fully prepared for the interest that the topic of diversity would stimulate or the enormous attention it now routinely receives in both the private and public sectors. Throughout the 70s and 80s, I was hopeful that my work and the work of those few dedicated colleagues who formed the nucleus of the valuing diversity movement would encourage more people to take an active interest in exploring the "differences that make a difference." But I never fathomed that a whole new industry of diversity consultants would be born in the 1990s or that organizations would be hiring public relations firms to highlight their valuing diversity efforts and creating new internal hierarchies to manage them.

In assessing the valuing diversity movement over the past 10 years, one can take satisfaction in the significant progress that has been made. At the most fundamental level, diversity is now a mainstream topic. It no longer stands on the periphery of organizational life in America. As a result of this movement into mainstream consciousness, it is now commonplace to find people engaging in discussions and celebrations of diversity in communities and organizations throughout the United States. More importantly, it is now difficult to find executives and managers who have not been exposed to the topic of "managing a culturally diverse workforce" in at least one conference, seminar, speech, or workshop.

But while awareness of diversity has increased dramatically during the last decade, there are also disturbing signs that its promise has not yet been fully realized and that the movement that spawned the term *valuing diversity* is beginning to derail. With increasing frequency, articles are appearing in major newspapers and business publications criticizing diversity programs and describing a growing backlash among "mainstream" workers. Because of the enormous public interest in diversity and the missteps that have already occurred, it is no exaggeration to say that the valuing diversity movement now stands at an important crossroads. The choices that are made now and the course of action that is set will determine its ultimate success or failure.

Today, the myriad training programs, planning councils, diversity audits, consultants, and organization initiatives that purport to be changing corporate cultures often seem to be focused more on generating activity than results. While awareness and understanding have become a staple of every organization's diversity strategy, many programs to increase awareness appear to be generating more heat but not more light. While diversity advocates talk about inclusion as critical for effective implementation, their actions and principal message often exclude select groups. While some organizations distinguish between affirmative action and valuing diversity, many others have blurred the lines between these two distinctly different initiatives and, in so doing, increased confusion and resistance among most employees. Finally, while the business case for diversity grows stronger with shifting U.S. demographics and increased globalization, many organizations have yet to link diversity with their business strategies—choosing instead to isolate the topic and to treat it as another human resources program.

This book takes a close look at a broad spectrum of organizational efforts made to date to value diversity. The case histories and examples used in each chapter are drawn from a rich variety of corporate, government, and academic settings. Because it is a critical analysis of both the classic missteps and the limited successes that have occurred, the names of the organizations and principles involved have been omitted; for the purpose is not to blame but instead to call attention to the emerging patterns, both productive and alarming, that are now taking shape on the valuing diversity landscape.

In many ways, this book could not have been written earlier, when the valuing diversity movement was in its infancy; however with the benefit of hindsight and experience, it is now possible to identify both the patterns of success and the missteps that are occurring as more organizations move to address the issues and pursue the opportunities that implementing diversity offers. *It is critical that we learn from these experiences and refine our approaches based on this ongoing feedback.*

In challenging several popular assumptions about diversity implementation, this book suggests it may now be time for a course correction; for despite the efforts of many public and private organizations over the last decade, we have yet to engage most Americans in the implementation of this important change. While we have gotten their attention, we have not yet motivated many in the mainstream to join us on this journey.

Implementing Diversity is being written with two audiences in mind. First, it is a wake-up call for managers and diversity specialists who have been working to change cultures and who are not completely satisfied with the success of their organizations' implementation efforts. By analyzing a variety of implementation case histories described in this book, experienced agents of change can increase their understanding of the emerging patterns of resistance and support that are building within organizations and develop new, more creative strategies to deal with both.

This book is also being written for people who value diversity, who believe in its potential, and who are just beginning to help their organizations change in order to support it. Many of the classic mistakes outlined in these pages could not have been anticipated or easily avoided by those leading-edge organizations that were out there first. However, if they are recognized and anticipated, these barriers to implementation can now be minimized by managers and organizations in the early stages of change or about to begin the journey.

To aid in this process, *Implementing Diversity* has been divided into three sections. Section I, "Going Back to Basics" begins with a self-assessment exercise that helps one gauge where an organization currently stands in its efforts to implement diversity. It then provides a brief history of the valuing diversity movement and a concise summary of change management principles that can accelerate adoption of the value of diversity. Section II, "Barriers to Implementation" offers an in-depth look at the serious problems and stumbling blocks that regularly surface during diversity implementation and now threaten the success of many corporate programs. Section III, "Accelerating Change," details a comprehensive plan for overcoming the barriers, improving receptivity, and achieving long-term, lasting success.

Finally, this book will make demands on its readers that other diversity books do not. Its format has been designed to be interactive. Through a series of case studies and questions about implementation issues, this book will challenge the reader to get involved rather than remain passive. By analyzing a variety of implementation case histories described in these pages, the reader will become familiar with the classic missteps that are now being made in many organizations. As a result, it will then be easier to avoid these problems, accelerate change, and broaden support for the value of diversity.

Today, our planet is beset by increasing problems and tensions. To fully understand and overcome these enormous difficulties, we will need to tap the talents of every human being. Viewed from this perspective, valuing diversity is not just of vital importance to business, but it is of critical importance to our global society. To secure our future, it is a vision that must be fulfilled and a goal that must be accomplished. For those of us who welcome this change, it is now time to plot a course that will help assure ultimate success.

CONTENTS

Going Back to Basics

ONE

Taking Stock

Those of us engaged in the work of implementing diversity in organizations know that it is an exciting and challenging undertaking. Because implementation usually involves some fundamental culture change, it often takes several years to accomplish. As we become caught up in the particular issues and challenges of the change process, it is sometimes easy to lose sight of where the organization stands relative to the long-term goals and objectives of the overall valuing diversity effort.

This chapter is designed to help you step back and assess the current vitality of your organization's diversity implementation efforts. By answering a series of questions about your organization's current implementation effort, you will be able to identify major problem areas that now exist that could cause your organization's diversity program to veer off course—if no remedial action is taken. *If you are working in an organization that has an ongoing diversity program or process, answer each question in Section A of this chapter as it pertains to valuing diversity within your organization.* If a particular question is not applicable, skip it and move on. Pay particular attention to those statements to which you answer yes.

If you are in an organization that is just beginning to design an implementation plan, refer to Section B of this chapter. Again, answer each question based on your understanding of your organization's start-up implementation process. Pay particular attention to those statements to which you answer no.

3

SECTION A: ONGOING IMPLEMENTATION ASSESSMENT

Within Your Organization . . .

- Is there growing resistance to valuing diversity efforts?

    ☐ Yes   ☐ No

- Is valuing diversity confused with affirmative action?

    ☐ Yes   ☐ No

- Do people use phrases like "diverse person" and "diversity hire" when referring only to women and/or people of color?

    ☐ Yes   ☐ No

- Do many white men feel excluded from the valuing diversity effort?

    ☐ Yes   ☐ No

- Is prejudice reduction or diversity awareness training mandatory for employees?

    ☐ Yes   ☐ No

- Is turnover higher for particular groups based upon differences such as age, gender, race, and sexual orientation?

    ☐ Yes   ☐ No

- Are managers who do not demonstrate that they value diversity promoted and rewarded?

    ☐ Yes   ☐ No

- Is the strategic business case for valuing diversity unclear to many employees?

    ☐ Yes   ☐ No

- Is awareness training available for managers but not for employees?

    ☐ Yes   ☐ No

- Is awareness training the only visible corporate initiative aimed at valuing diversity?

  ☐ Yes   ☐ No

- Are actual EO profile and promotion statistics unpublished and unavailable to most employees?

  ☐ Yes   ☐ No

- Does the human resources department have primary responsibility for implementing diversity?

  ☐ Yes   ☐ No

- Are external consultants used exclusively to facilitate diversity awareness training?

  ☐ Yes   ☐ No

- Do employee networks/affinity groups appear isolated, competitive, and/or divisive?

  ☐ Yes   ☐ No

- Do most managers fail to see diversity as having an impact on productivity, profitability, and service?

  ☐ Yes   ☐ No

- Based upon employee profile demographics, is your organization less than truly diverse at all levels?

  ☐ Yes   ☐ No

- Do particular groups of employees believe that there is still a glass ceiling?

  ☐ Yes   ☐ No

- Do senior executives show little interest in and active support for the value of diversity?

  ☐ Yes   ☐ No

If you answered yes to more than two of the above statements, it may be time to reassess the effectiveness of your company's ongoing diversity implementation efforts. Each statement in this survey describes an issue or problem that can occur during implementation of diversity initiatives. While these issues can occur in isolation, they often occur simultaneously and can slow implementation and even stop adoption of the value of diversity when they arise.

As you review your *yes* responses, ask yourself how serious these issues are. Do they threaten the overall success of diversity implementation in your company? Has your organization instituted corrective measures to address each problem? Based upon your involvement to date, are you completely satisfied with the way diversity is being implemented within your organization now? If you think there is room for improvement or a need to reinvigorate your organization's valuing diversity effort, you will be taking an important step towards enhancing effectiveness by reading this book. You can begin to be more proactive now by turning to Chapter 2.

SECTION B: START-UP IMPLEMENTATION ASSESSMENT

This assessment is for individuals working in organizations that are just beginning to implement a valuing diversity initiative. If the topic of diversity has only recently begun to get attention and most managers and employees have yet to receive any education or training to support the diversity effort, the following assessment probably applies to your organization.

Within Your Organization . . .

- Is the discussion of valuing diversity being driven by bottom-line objectives?

    ☐ Yes   ☐ No

- Do executives recognize the need for culture change in order to succeed with diversity?

    ☐ Yes   ☐ No

- Has industry benchmarking of diversity efforts in other organizations been done?

  ☐ Yes   ☐ No

- Has a highly diverse start-up team responsible for strategy development and implementation planning been formed?

  ☐ Yes   ☐ No

- If so, is the team's size between 8 and 12 individuals?

  ☐ Yes   ☐ No

- Has the start-up team received extensive diversity awareness training?

  ☐ Yes   ☐ No

- Does the start-up team include individuals with organization development and change management experience?

  ☐ Yes   ☐ No

- If not, is an experienced organization change consultant working with this group?

  ☐ Yes   ☐ No

- Has the start-up team participated in team building?

  ☐ Yes   ☐ No

- Does the start-up team have a diversity definition, vision, and written strategic plan to guide its work?

  ☐ Yes   ☐ No

- Does the start-up team have ongoing access to senior management regarding diversity implementation?

  ☐ Yes   ☐ No

- Has a cultural assessment been completed?

  ☐ Yes   ☐ No

- If not, is one now being planned?

  ☐ Yes   ☐ No

- Is there an adequate multiyear budget to support a comprehensive valuing diversity initiative?

  ☐ Yes   ☐ No

- Have senior managers and key influencers with a strong interest in valuing diversity been identified and/or cultivated?

  ☐ Yes   ☐ No

- Has an ongoing stewardship role been defined for members of this important subgroup?

  ☐ Yes   ☐ No

- Have all senior managers participated in diversity leadership training?

  ☐ Yes   ☐ No

- Were all the steps outlined in this assessment taken prior to design and delivery of employee diversity awareness training?

  ☐ Yes   ☐ No

Each statement in this survey describes an important early step that should be taken to assure success in implementing diversity programs and processes. *If you answered no to more than two of the statements in this assessment, your organization's diversity initiative may be getting off to a less-than-optimal start.* Successful diversity implementation depends upon a strong foundation of benchmarking, start-up planning, and organization climate assessment. Success also requires active stewardship by those leaders and key influencers who recognize the value that diversity offers. If your organization's start-up efforts are not grounded by these four key elements: benchmarking, planning, climate assessment, and leadership involvement, they are less likely to succeed at changing the culture and institutionalizing the value of diversity.

This book is an informational resource that can help you avoid many missteps as you successfully guide the implementation process. Throughout the book, a series of case histories will be presented, outlining many implementation problems that slow down the adoption of diversity as well as best practices that are enabling some companies to begin succeeding through diversity. By understanding both the classic errors and successful practices that are occurring in many organizational diversity efforts now in progress, you will be in a better position to help accelerate implementation of diversity in your organization while minimizing conflict and confusion along the way. Turn now to Chapter 2 and may you have an exciting and successful journey!

TWO

Defining Diversity

The following is a brief case history of one company's ill-fated attempt to define diversity and build support for implementation. As you read through the case, consider what could have been done differently to assure a more successful outcome.

THE COO's SPEECH

A prominent software development company determined that it was time to begin a highly visible organizationwide effort to value diversity. This decision was made by the executive staff immediately after the software company was acquired by a larger organization immersed in diversity culture change.

To kick off this effort, the organization planned a multiday diversity conference to be hosted at one of its large manufacturing facilities. Invitations were sent to over 300 employees from every plant location throughout the United States as well as to human resources specialists, select corporate executives, and middle-level operations managers. In addition, management representatives from facilities in Europe, Asia, and Latin America were invited to attend.

A multilevel, multicultural planning committee was convened to design the four-day experience and an elaborate agenda with panels and concurrent workshops resulted. Finally, the date of the oversubscribed event arrived, and managers and employees gathered to hear about the organization's newest strategic thrust—valuing diversity. To help lay out the company's plan, the keynote address on the first day was delivered by the organization's chief operating officer, a man highly respected by many employees in the company with a reputation for being a "smart, fair, and empowering manager."

As he began his remarks, elaborate charts and graphs appeared on the projection screens. Each one depicted the race/gender profile of a particular level of management in the software subsidiary. The first part of the presentation focused on the current race/gender profile of the organization, which, not surprisingly, was predominantly white and male at the top. The conclusion showed how that profile would be changed over the course of the next five years through accelerated advancement for women and people of color as well as through voluntary attrition and "right sizing." At the conclusion of his speech, the COO remarked that this was the most aggressive valuing diversity plan ever developed in the organization and that he certainly hoped everyone present would help him achieve it in the months and years to come.

Following his closing comments, the meeting was adjourned for the day. The next morning a series of workshops was presented on a variety of topics including cross-cultural communication, interviewing skills, conflict resolution, introduction to dialogue, and so on. While the topics varied greatly, it seemed the responses from many in the audience did not. Regardless of the focus of the workshops, the facilitators noticed that conferees continued to refer back to the COO's speech. Many comments were made about how "unfair" the company's diversity plan was. There was also much heated discussion about "reverse discrimination" and how diversity threatened to "lower performance standards." Although never directly addressed, these themes continued to echo throughout the remaining three days of the meeting. As the conference continued, attendance fell off. By the fourth day, fewer than 150 people showed up. Most of the people missing were managers, many of whom were white men. The majority of those still present were women and people of color.

Key Questions:

1. If you were attending this conference, what definition of diversity might you have come away with after listening to the COO's keynote address?

2. Was the plan described in the keynote address a "valuing diversity plan"?

3. If you happened to be a white man attending this conference, would you have felt included in the discussion of the company's diversity plan?

4. As a manager or diversity specialist, do you think the opinions of white men matter when implementation is being planned? Should white men be included in valuing diversity efforts?

After a presentation like the one described above, it is not unusual for many employees to go from "bullish" to "bearish" on diversity. While keynote addresses from senior management can communicate executive support and commitment in the early stages of implementation, such talks can also foster resistance to change if diversity is defined too narrowly. To avoid widescale opposition, diversity must be defined in a broad and inclusive way. The corporate definition must make it obvious to employees at all levels that *everyone* is included and therefore *everyone's* diversity is valued.

Diversity Includes Everyone

Although the point may seem obvious, organizations often send out confusing signals to employees in the early stages of implementation. In many companies, the scene described in the preceding case history often repeats itself again and again, building resistance rather than support, until the backlash against diversity literally overpowers the effort.

Companies' inherent biases about diversity are often reflected in the way it is positioned and defined by executives. When executives have not internalized the important message that diversity includes everyone, their comments frequently imply that "white males

Implementation Principle #1:

To avoid widescale opposition, diversity must be defined in a broad and inclusive way. The definition must make it obvious to employees that everyone is included and therefore everyone's diversity is valued.

need not apply." In many institutions, diversity seems to pertain only to women and people of color; hence, a diverse person in such an organization can not be a white man.

In other cases, diversity is used as shorthand for a variety of characteristics such as learning style, individual thinking style, and so on, but is seldom used to refer to differences such as age, gender, physical abilities, sexual orientation, or race. In each case, the definitions are less encompassing than they need to be to address the complex issues and real opportunities that diversity represents in today's workplace and marketplace.

The Dimensions of Diversity[1]

Like trees in a vast forest, humans come in a variety of sizes, shapes, and colors. This variety helps to differentiate us. While we share the important dimension of humanness with all members of our species, there are biological and environmental differences that separate and distinguish us as individuals and groups. It is this vast array of physical and cultural differences that constitute the spectrum of human diversity.

Given the myriad ways in which we are different, how do we arrive at a broad, workable, workplace definition that is inclusive but not overwhelmingly so? We do this by including in our definition *those important human characteristics that impact individuals' values, opportunities, and perceptions of self and others at work* and by highlighting how individuals aggregate into larger subgroups based upon shared characteristics. Using these criteria, a workplace definition of diversity would minimally include:

- Age.
- Ethnicity.
- Gender.
- Mental/physical abilities and characteristics.
- Race.
- Sexual orientation.

Primary and Secondary Dimensions of Diversity

These six differences are termed *core dimensions of diversity* because they exert an important impact on our early socialization and a powerful, sustained impact throughout every stage of life. Like interlocking segments of a sphere, *these six dimensions represent properties and characteristics that constitute the core of our diverse identities.* All individuals have a variety of dimensions of diversity through which they experience the world and by which they are defined. At the core of each of us, there are these six at minimum.

For some individuals there may be a seventh and even an eighth dimension of diversity included in the core; for example, religion is a core difference for some, but not for all individuals, because of the powerful, sustaining impact that it exerts throughout some individuals' lives. In defining core dimensions, it is the immutability and sustained power that certain dimensions exert throughout life that separates them from other important secondary dimensions.

Beyond the six core dimensions already discussed, there are many secondary dimensions that play an important role in shaping our values, expectations, and experiences as well. These include:

- Communication style.
- Education.
- Family status.
- Military experience.
- Organizational role and level.
- Religion.
- First language.
- Geographic location.
- Income.
- Work experience.
- Work style.

Like the core dimensions, these *secondary dimensions* share certain characteristics. Generally, they *are more mutable, less visible to others around us, and more variable in the degree of influence they exert on our individual lives.* Many secondary dimensions contain an element of control or choice. Because we acquire, discard, and modify these dimensions, their power is less constant and more individualized than is true for the core dimensions. Yet despite the fact that these dimensions have less life-long influence, most individuals are more conscious of their impact at a given point in time than they are regarding primary dimensions. They are more

likely to appreciate the cause-and-effect relationships that exist
between these secondary dimensions of diversity and events in their
own lives.

The Diversity Wheel

The following diagram illustrates both the primary and secondary
dimensions of diversity that exert an impact on us in the workplace
as well as in society. While each dimension adds a layer of
complexity, it is the dynamic interaction among all the dimensions
of diversity that influences one's self-image, values, opportunities,
and expectations. Together, the primary and secondary dimensions
give definition and meaning to our lives by contributing to a
synergistic, integrated whole—the diverse person.

Dimensions of Diversity

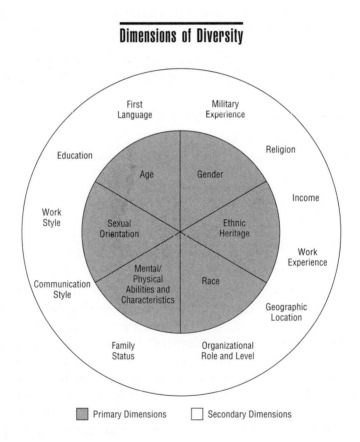

Core Dimensions: A Constant Influence

While core dimensions exert a powerful influence throughout our lifetime, many people are unaware of the ways in which these differences matter. For example, regardless of whether you are currently age 20, 30, 50, or over 60, your age has a bearing on how you are perceived by others as well as on your ability to learn, relate to your environment, and contribute at work. No matter what age group you fall into, your age is a key factor in shaping your opportunities.

When the perceptions and expectations that others have of you as a person of a particular age are closely aligned with your own, then this dimension of your diversity is less likely to be one that is associated with conflict in the workplace. While it nonetheless remains a core dimension and exerts a continuous impact, age would be considered a dimension in the background, adding another layer of complexity to who you are and how you see the world without stimulating internal or interpersonal conflict.

During those periods in life when particular core dimensions are part of the background and not in the foreground, people often lose consciousness of how they continue to influence assumptions, expectations, and opportunities. At such times we may even diminish their importance, arguing that core dimensions really don't matter all that much. Because they are so basic to who we are as human beings, we can lose sight of their importance until our particular circumstances change. When we face conflicts between our self-perceptions, our expectations, and the perceptions of others based on a core dimension of our diversity, we are suddenly reminded that basic differences *do* matter. It is during these periods of conflict that we often become more aware of the ways in which biases about core dimensions of our diversity can impede our progress.

Core Dimensions and Unearned Privilege

With the possible exception of ethnic heritage, this pattern of less consciousness regarding the impact of core dimensions during periods of prosperity or reduced conflict and greater awareness as a result of heightened negative attention remain consistent for most people in most situations. Why? Perhaps it is our culture's emphasis on rugged individualism that obscures the importance of these basic differences. Many people in our culture are uncomfortable attributing any positive or negative occurrences to their age, gender, race, and so on. They prefer to see themselves as individuals with an equal chance to succeed and will minimize the significance of core dimensions and their memberships in these different groups. In addition, the unearned advantages that we can derive by dint of being born into certain subgroups are often not in our consciousness. When they are called to our attention, we may reject the idea that our age, skin color, gender, physical abilities, or sexual orientation could give us unearned privileges or serve as advantages in competitive situations where diversity is not valued.

While these advantages may be apparent to people outside of the privileged group(s) to which we may belong, those of us who attain more immediate credibility due to our age, gender, race, physical abilities, or presumed sexual orientation are seldom aware of how our core identities influence our opportunities and enhance our status. Perhaps it is just too painful to acknowledge that we are not living in a true meritocracy and accept the fact that one's accomplishments can be due in part to unearned privileges arbitrarily awarded on the basis of gender, race, age, and so on, rather than on the basis of individual ability.

Organizations intent on creating cultures that value diversity recognize the importance of rewarding employees for their achievements. They avoid re-creating the patterns in differential status and access that were created when privileges were assigned based upon age, skin color, gender, sexual orientation, and so on, and work to assure that the core identities of all employees are recognized and respected.

Creating Awareness of the Impact of Core Dimensions

One of the critical challenges of implementing diversity is helping individuals appreciate how core differences like age, gender, race, and mental and physical abilities *do* matter—a task that is often difficult to accomplish due to widespread reluctance to acknowledge how core differences helped to create hierarchies of privilege. But while this is a difficult topic to explore, the recognition of this hierarchy can be the first step towards valuing diversity. For it is only after we appreciate the subtle ways in which one's core identity can help open doors to opportunity—while others with different core identities remain locked out—that we can resolve to value all core identities equally and create a truly level playing field on which to compete and succeed.

THREE

EEO, Affirmative Action, and Valuing Diversity

How is valuing diversity different from equal employment opportunity (EEO) and affirmative action (AA) programs? Without exception, one can anticipate that this question will be asked repeatedly throughout an organization during the early stages of diversity implementation.

In answering this question, it is important to remember that equal employment law and affirmative action focus on preventing and/or correcting discriminatory employment practices that impact workforce representation. Valuing diversity is an outgrowth of these efforts, but it is also a qualitatively different concept. It goes a step beyond mere numbers and seeks to maximize the potential of every individual. Together, EEO, AA, and valuing diversity play an integral part in helping organizations create a level playing field *and* an environment that supports and leverages the talents of all employees.

EEO Background

Since the early 1960s, a number of federally sponsored equal employment laws have been enacted prohibiting workplace discrimination based on age, color, disability, Vietnam era veteran status, national origin, race, religion, and sex. While these EEO laws encourage nondiscrimination based on certain dimensions of diversity, they offer no specific guidelines for correcting historic patterns of exclusion and discrimination when these are found within an organization.

To address these discriminatory patterns in organizations, affirmative action programs were subsequently put into place. Generally, such programs are built upon the assumption that lifting discriminatory barriers does not automatically create a level playing field on which to compete for opportunities. Because of historic patterns of discrimination, some proactive steps may first be required to help close the gap. Most affirmative action programs aim at closing gaps by setting targets and timetables to change the race/gender profile in specific job categories within an organization. They can therefore be termed profile improvement programs.

While all affirmative action programs are also profile improvement programs, the reverse is not true. In companies that do not fall under the jurisdiction of the Office of Federal Contract Compliance (OFCCP), affirmative action programs are not mandated. Nonetheless, in many such organizations, profile improvement programs have been created internally to replicate the effects of affirmative action. While these programs are not audited by the government to assure compliance, they are typically concerned with race/gender profile improvement and are usually monitored by internal EEO managers.

Regardless of whether they are mandated by the federal government or not, all profile improvement programs look at demographic trends in the workplace and society and try to more closely match an organization's employee profile to that of the external labor pool. Since affirmative action programs began in the early 1970s, they have been credited in virtually every organization where they exist with increasing access for women and people of color to many nontraditional jobs—positions that typically paid more and had better career potential than those jobs traditionally held by members of these groups.

Affirmative Action Today

Today, more than 20 years after the first affirmative action program was implemented in a U.S. corporation, there are some in our society who think the time has come to put an end to such efforts. As job security continues to disappear for many Americans and the U.S. economy continues to falter, affirmative action has become a lightning rod for some politicians and talk show hosts eager to stir public debate, play on people's fears, win votes, or boost ratings. In California, the bellwether state for many national movements, there is an initiative on the ballot to repeal affirmative action in state agencies. As this book goes to press, similar proposals are being put forward in other states, and debate about the future of affirmative action at the federal level is already beginning in the U.S. Congress.

While the politics of division make dramatic headlines, most of the accusations about rigid, unfair quotas and reverse discrimination have nothing to do with the reality of profile improvement efforts in most U.S. organizations. Despite rumors to the contrary, white men are far from becoming an endangered species in the American workplace of the 1990s. In fact, in a 1995 study conducted by a bipartisan U.S. congressional committee, this group was found to hold 95 percent of senior management positions in industry despite the fact that they represent 43 percent of the American workforce. According to the same study, despite three decades of affirmative action, glass ceilings were still firmly in place for women and people of color above middle-management levels.[1]

Can organizations value diversity *without* affirmative action or, more broadly speaking, without profile improvement in the 1990s? While it is certainly feasible to evolve to a point where such improvement is no longer needed, most companies are simply not there yet. In order to value diversity, institutions must first assure that they are *truly diverse* at every level—not just when it comes to the secondary dimensions, but diverse in terms of the primary dimensions of diversity as well. Without a specific plan focused on hiring, training, and promoting underrepresented groups, many organizations would continue to fall short of this goal; thus, it seems that affirmative action still has a role to play in helping organizations first recognize and then develop underutilized talent. But while it can play a critical role during the early stages of diversity implementation, changing the employee profile is *not* synonymous with valuing diversity. In fact, it is entirely possible to have great cultural diversity represented in an organization's workforce, but not value the differences or leverage the potential that greater cultural diversity offers. Thus, valuing diversity and diversity per se are not the same thing.

Differences between EEO/AA and Valuing Diversity

When companies work to value diversity, they move beyond profile improvement that is focused solely on race and gender. Now the focus becomes the corporate environment and the degree to which it is welcoming and rewarding for *everyone*. The goal is no longer merely satisfying legal requirements; instead, it now expands to include correcting environmental issues, improving productivity, and enhancing employee morale.

By focusing on the quality of the work environment and on the full utilization of the skills of *all* employees, valuing diversity takes a giant step beyond affirmative action. Its message of inclusion and respect can defuse the residue of confusion, resentment, and backlash that are occurring today in many organizations due in large part to our sluggish economy, massive corporate downsizing, the politics of division, and, in some cases, poorly executed affirmative action programs.

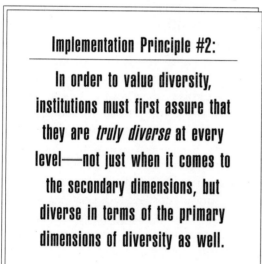

Implementation Principle #2:

In order to value diversity, institutions must first assure that they are *truly diverse* at every level—not just when it comes to the secondary dimensions, but diverse in terms of the primary dimensions of diversity as well.

While profile improvement may still be a requirement, under the canopy of valuing diversity, it can now be positioned as serving the organization's increased need for innovation, multicultural marketing, effective teamwork, and so on. As a new management paradigm, valuing diversity holds organizations accountable for creating cultures in which diversity thrives and for fully utilizing the diverse talents of every employee. It presumes that with reasonable modifications in organizational assumptions, systems, and practices, this diversity in talent can be better leveraged for enhanced productivity and competitive advantage.

While one can see overlap in the goals of EEO/AA programs and valuing diversity initiatives, it is important to recognize how these efforts differ. The following chart describes some of the key differences between these important thrusts:

EEO/Affirmative Action	Valuing Diversity
Quantitative: Focused on demographic profile change.	*Qualitative:* Focused on environmental readiness.
Government Mandated: Imposed and often unwelcomed.	*Voluntary:* Internally driven and welcomed.
Remedial: Focused on changing historic patterns of discrimination.	*Strategic:* Focused on increasing innovation and creating competitive advantage.
Reactive: Problem response.	*Proactive:* Opportunity-driven.
Beneficiaries: Protected groups.	*Beneficiaries:* Everyone
Initial Step.	*Follow-up Step.*
Culture Change *Not Required.*	Culture Change *Required.*

In many respects, valuing diversity is an innovation that grew out of early EEO/AA efforts to end discrimination and thereby end exclusion. It is a follow-up step that many organizations initiate after some internal profile changes have already occurred. The basic aim of valuing diversity is to create a more flexible, diversity-friendly environment where the talents of all employees can flourish and be leveraged for individual, work team, and organizational success.

Instead of ignoring cultural differences, valuing diversity efforts encourage all members of the organization to increase their knowledge about diverse cultures and to share information about their core identities. Valuing diversity initiatives focus on bridging gaps in respect and understanding that exist among different cultural groups and on creating a workplace atmosphere of increased comfort, empathy, and common ground for all employees. While all of this helps organizations assure that diversity becomes a competitive advantage, none of it is required to achieve the numeric goals of typical affirmative action and profile improvement programs.

While the objectives of EEO/AA and valuing diversity are complementary, they can wind up on a collision course if the purpose of each is not made clear within an organization. Consider the following example:

NEW PACKAGING . . . OLD MESSAGE

Harriet Marshall is the EEO and diversity manager for a large division of a prominent office equipment manufacturing company. When she took the position 15 years ago, the company had just paid out several million dollars in damages due to a sex discrimination suit brought against it by several women engineers and technicians. After paying more than $4 million in damages, the company had signed a consent decree to protect itself from further class action suits. As part of this decree, it agreed to develop a plan to accelerate advancement for women within the organization and appointed Harriet to manage EEO/AA matters.

Over the past 10 years, Harriet has seen the company make strides in hiring larger numbers of women into technical jobs and advancing more women from entry-level positions to middle management. She has also noticed that most of the promotion opportunities that have resulted from the company's affirmative action program have gone to white women. Today, there are still few people of color in engineering positions in the company and therefore few in the pipeline for promotion to key operating positions in management.

Harriet believes an aggressive profile improvement effort will be required to change the racial demographics of the organization. She also senses that senior management is less focused on encouraging profile improvement, particularly since the company began a major cost reduction and downsizing effort last year.

In order to rekindle interest and create greater management support, Harriet recently convened a global diversity council to help the organization begin implementation of a valuing diversity initiative. The team's stated mission is to "facilitate the organization's cultural transformation so that diversity becomes a competitive advantage."

After several meetings to identify priorities, the council developed three stretch goals that it hopes to achieve over the next five years. They include:

- Create an employee profile that matches the civilian labor pool.

- Shatter the glass ceiling at middle-management levels for employees of color.

- Increase company purchases from women and minority-owned businesses by 20 percent.

In an effort to communicate to all employees about the valuing diversity initiative, the council was recently interviewed in the company's employee newsletter. A sidebar to the article featured its three stretch goals.

While Harriet is pleased to have the council's support, she is disappointed in the organization's response to the article publicizing its work. Since it ran, several managers have asked her how the group's work differs from the company's affirmative action program. When she explains that the group is about facilitating culture change, discussion usually stops. But she continues to hear comments like "There's nothing new here," when she visits the company's manufacturing facilities to talk about valuing diversity with employees.

Based upon the verbal feedback she has received so far, Harriet senses that there is growing apathy and even resistance among managers and employees to the work of the diversity council. She also believes this will change once the executive staff "buys in" to the team's stretch goals.

Key Questions:

1. Given the diversity council's stated mission, are its three stretch goals comprehensive enough?

2. In addition to publicizing the goals, what else should the council do to build support for its work among employees and managers?

3. Is the EEO manager the most appropriate person in an organization to lead a corporate valuing diversity effort? Who else might be appropriate?

4. What could Harriet do to broaden her own understanding of the scope of the valuing diversity initiative?

In many organizations profile improvement is still a critical component of a comprehensive valuing diversity implementation. However, *when it is presented as the heart of the valuing diversity culture change, profile improvement can create a barrier to acceptance* among those employees who see it as nothing new—a repackaging of affirmative action in a different wrapper.

To gain broad support, the message of valuing diversity must make it clear to all employees that the initiative goes well beyond affirmative action and is aimed at creating a more cooperative, inclusive, innovative, and productive work environment for all. Employees at all levels must see some personal as well as organizational benefit before they can be expected to buy in.

Today a repackaging of profile improvement goals is occurring in many companies as references to affirmative action disappear and talk turns to valuing diversity; but regardless of what it is called, profile improvement alone will not change the corporate culture or assure that diversity is respected and leveraged. This will only occur after a comprehensive set of actions are implemented tying diversity's value to strategic business goals and enhancing the flexibility and openness of the corporate culture. Until that time, talk about valuing diversity is likely to be just that.

Developing a comprehensive implementation plan to institutionalize the value of diversity demands that the architects of the plan step out of the familiar box. While some "tried and true" methods such as affirmative action may still be appropriate, the paradigm shift from assimilating to valuing differences requires new approaches to change management as well as a redefinition of both the problems and opportunities. Managers and diversity specialists who support culture change must be willing to question their own assumptions about what it will take to get there. When they remain open to evolving their ideas and their approach, many discover that some fundamental beliefs about what valuing diversity is and how to achieve it are among the first items to change.

FOUR

Valuing Diversity: Program or New Paradigm?

s with many ideas that carry potential for increased innovation and improved productivity, valuing diversity can have a dramatic impact on an organization's functioning or wind up becoming the "program of the month." How it is viewed at the outset of implementation can often have a great influence on the breadth and depth of its long-term impact. Once again, the self-fulfilling prophesy is very much in evidence. Consider the following scenario:

THE CONSULTING CONUNDRUM

During 1992 two competing consulting firms decided to begin diversity implementations in the same quarter. Firm A, regarded in the industry as "extremely successful and very conservative," was committed to attracting a broader, more diverse candidate pool from which to hire analysts and junior associates. The reason behind this interest was the firm's increasingly diverse client base.

During 1991, several corporate clients had begun to request that diverse consulting teams be assigned to work on their projects. Minimally, this usually meant including one or two women or people of color. Since fewer than 10 percent of Firm A's professional staff were women and less than 5 percent were people of color, the company was interested in "casting a wider net" through recruitment efforts in order to address this deficiency.

To do this, Firm A decided to include several tier two business schools on its campus recruiting list for the first time in its history. While tier two schools consistently rated in the top 20 percent of U.S. graduate business schools, Firm A did not regard these schools as equal to tier one schools. However, tier two schools did have larger enrollments of women and people of color.

Firm B also determined that the demographics of its professional staff no longer matched with client desires. In a similar effort, Firm B went to work to enhance its diversity-friendly image as a prospective employer for women and people of color by changing its recruitment brochures, annual report, and so forth, to show more examples of women, people of color, and people with disabilities in professional roles.

Firm B also decided to begin recruiting at several business schools with larger enrollments of women and people of color. Finally, it developed a two-year summer intern program and designated half of the 10 places in the three-month orientation for women and people of color.

After 18 months, Firm A had interviewed more than 150 candidates and had hired 20 women and people of color. During their initial year at the firm, no particular attention was given to helping the new hires adjust to their environment. On the contrary, since several partners believed that special treatment for women and people of color would be unfair, no efforts were made to help orient the new hires to the firm and its highly competitive culture. As one senior associate stated, "This has always been a sink-or-swim environment. No one is going to throw you a life jacket."

A year later, only one person from the original group of 20 hires remained. This unusually rapid turnover prompted one partner to state, "It's time to return to our tried-and-true hiring methods. In the future, we shouldn't allow our clients to pressure us into lowering our standards. Look what happens when we bow to that kind of demand."

At Firm B, 30 women and people of color were hired along with 50 white men from tier one and two graduate business schools. Immediately following their initial training, each new hire was assigned a managing mentor to serve as a performance coach and informational resource. All mentors were given cultural awareness training and performance-coaching skills training to help them succeed in their new role.

An associate "buddy system" was also started and each new hire was paired with one second- or third-year associate who shared similar hobbies and interests. The purpose of this informal pairing was to provide each new associate with a peer who could introduce him or her to the external community, help with relocation questions and concerns, interact socially, and be a link to other associates at the firm. Despite a rigorous initial training program comparable to that at Firm A, turnover for all new hires after one year was approximately 20 percent. This percentage remained consistent across all race and gender groups.

After two years, the original number at Firm B had been reduced by 30 percent with 20 women and people of color and 35 white men remaining. This rate of attrition was 5 to 10 percent lower than in prior years. At the same time, in an effort to support greater work/family balance among employees, Firm B decided to develop a part-time partner track for associates. Two larger offices in major urban areas also became involved in on-site child care programs that all employees were invited to utilize.

Throughout the two-year period, Firm B partners spoke frequently at staff meetings and company functions about their desire to enhance the work environment in order to make it more welcoming and supportive for all employees. At Firm A, nothing about diversity or culture change was ever discussed at staff meetings except when an outside speaker was brought in for a Friday lunch presentation.

Key Questions:

1. Which of the two firms described in this case remind you more of your own organization? Would you say your company views diversity more as a short-term program or as a culture change?

2. What critical elements were present in Firm B's implementation that were missing from Firm A's?

3. What do you think is a reasonable time frame in which to achieve fundamental culture change?

This case history contrasts the short-term, quick-fix approach that some organizations take in their implementation efforts with a more comprehensive, systemic approach to valuing diversity. In the first example, no effort was directed at making the corporate environment more flexible or supportive. Instead, the firm's approach was to seek out different groups of people to introduce into the existing system by expanding the number of schools visited by its recruiters.

In the second example the company took a broader view. It concentrated on revamping its communications both internally and externally. It too expanded its recruitment efforts by including schools with larger populations of women and people of color. However, Firm B did not stop there. It also paid attention to the environment that all new people were expected to work in and took steps to assure that it was a welcoming and comfortable one by assigning every hire a mentor and a peer supporter. It also did not assume that all partners and directors were able to naturally manage a diverse workforce. Instead, the firm provided awareness and skill building for those managers being asked to play a coaching role. Finally, Firm B also worked to reduce the isolation that many newcomers feel in a new city and a new job before they find a friend or colleague with whom they share some personal interests.

While other actions could have been taken to augment this implementation, the contrast between the more systemic approach of Firm B and the sink-or-swim mentality of Firm A illustrates how diversity implementations can be distinctly different across organizations, even in the same industry. One major reason for this difference is the mindset that an organization employs in framing its implementation efforts. Where diversity is viewed as a problem requiring an immediate, quick-fix solution, implementation is likely to be programmatic and positive results more limited.

Until an organization recognizes valuing diversity as a new paradigm or new model for thinking about and managing human resources, it cannot fully recognize how assumptions, operating norms, systems, and practices must change in order to tap its potential. Once the paradigm shift and the fundamental systems changes occur, valuing diversity then becomes a source of vast creative possibility and enormous human potential.

Shifting the Paradigm

A comparison of today's more flexible, empowering, team-focused organization with the top-down, paramilitary model of the not-too-distant past illustrates how dramatically the concept of an effective organization has changed in the last 20 years in response to new technologies and increased competition. Now, U.S. organizations are changing again to accommodate rapidly shifting demographics in the labor force and in the global marketplace.

While cultural diversity is not new in U.S. society or the American workplace, until the 1980s it was not a significant factor in the way policies and practices were designed or expectations set in most institutions. Although diversity has always existed in the labor force, organizations managed it using a one-size-fits-all approach. As such, assimilating into the corporate environment was the responsibility of every employee. In return, treating all employees the same was the responsibility of every employer *and* was considered to be fair treatment by most.

Throughout the 1980s, patterns in attrition as well as employee feedback criticizing "inhospitable corporate cultures" helped create

Implementation Principle #3:

Leveraging diversity requires a fundamental shift in assumptions about the organization culture as well as changes in the basic systems and practices used to support customers and employees.

a new awareness in many organizations of the ways in which assimilation could diminish the potential of many employees and create invisible but very real barriers to their success. Thus, it became apparent that a more diverse employee mix did not assure that this increased diversity would be valued or leveraged. Leveraging diversity required a fundamental shift in assumptions about its benefit and in the systems and practices used to support customers and employees.

Since awareness of the need for culture change first became evident in U.S. organizations, many have begun the long journey from valuing sameness, assimilation, and a one-size-fits-all approach to employee and customer diversity towards the creation of cultures that are more flexible, open, and able to leverage the talents and perspectives of diverse groups. Today, as a result of increased awareness of the benefits that diversity offers, we see organizations at many points on the valuing diversity continuum. Some have remained traditional in their outlook, using a standardized approach to managing customer and employee diversity. They remain unconvinced that diversity can become a competitive advantage.

As organizations move up the continuum, diversity implementation is focused more on changes in basic norms, operating assumptions, and expectations. While a need for some assimilation regarding the organization's core values and fundamental mission continues, there is greater acceptance of diversity in styles and approaches to communication and problem solving. Once diversity becomes a desired asset, it is easy to recognize the ways in which operating assumptions and systems must change to achieve the end result. Now, valuing diversity is viewed as a fundamental part of the strategic business plan—not a stand-alone effort. While closely linked to human resources practices, valuing diversity is recognized as being more than an HR program. Rewards and recognition are tied to one's ability to value and leverage diversity. Marketing and sales programs and virtually all strategic business efforts are viewed through the lens of diversity, to assure that they reflect this core value.

Leaders of organizations moving up the continuum are also embarked on a personal journey. They recognize that increased knowledge of multicultural issues is critical for continued success. As such, they seek out opportunities to expand their multicultural knowledge, to become more self-aware, and to grow. They look for ways to mentor people different from themselves, challenge their peers to support diversity, and remain willing to take risks in order to move implementation forward.

Traditional Paradigm versus Valuing Diversity Paradigm

The following is a comparison of the traditional paradigm historically used in most organizations to manage diversity and the new paradigm built around diversity as a valued asset. The left column describes characteristics found in many organizations that manage diversity with a traditional, one-size-fits-all approach. The right column describes characteristics found in organizations that have made the paradigm shift and are on their way to creating cultures that value diversity. As you read through each list, keep in mind the current state of the diversity initiative in your organization.

Traditional paradigm	Valuing diversity paradigm
• Expectations, standards, and explicit and implicit rules shaped by the needs of those at the top.	• Expectations, standards, and explicit and implicit rules shaped by diverse customers and employees.
• Success linked to assimilation.	• Success linked to unique contribution.
• Limited range of appropriate communication, work, and leadership styles.	• Expanded range of styles.
• No strategic business linkage.	• Diversity is a competitive business strategy.
• Diversity equals a potential liability.	• Diversity equals a unique asset.
• No HR systems alignment.	• HR systems in alignment.
• No linkage to compensation and rewards.	• Strong linkage to compensation and rewards.
• Token gender and/or racial diversity at middle management levels.	• Visible diversity at all organizational levels.
• Uncommitted and uninformed leadership.	• Aware and committed leadership.
• Underlying assumption: Change the people and preserve the culture.	• Underlying assumption: Modify the culture to support the people.

Key Questions:

1. Where is your organization on the diversity continuum? (Select the appropriate number.)

   1   2   3   4   5   6   7

   1 = Very Traditional   7 = Fully Values Diversity

2. What two to three steps must be taken to move your organization farther up this continuum?

3. What specific steps can you take to help facilitate this change process?

Regardless of where your organization is today, it can continue to move up the continuum with help and support from those committed to change. Because valuing diversity is an innovation and a significant departure from status quo management methods, it takes more time and effort to introduce than one might initially expect. Obtaining organizational buy-in can take several years. It typically requires a reexamination of many cultural norms, expectations, and methods used to evaluate and manage performance.

To facilitate this reexamination, those who believe in the value of diversity must be sensitive to the impact of the current corporate culture on all diverse groups—not only those to which they themselves belong. They must recognize both the obvious and subtle ways in which organizational systems need modification to better leverage diversity. Once they understand what needs to be done, they must help others see the personal and organizational benefits of supporting these changes.

However, before we can correctly diagnose issues or help others support change, we must understand our own fundamental beliefs about valuing diversity. Have we made the paradigm shift within our own minds that allows us to think inclusively about this change? Are we ourselves prepared to do the long, difficult work required to modify the corporate culture, or are we looking for a quick, programmatic answer? Depending upon what mindset we bring to our work as facilitators of change, we will see diversity issues and opportunities quite differently.

If we view diversity as a short-term program for select groups, we will analyze every organizational issue and opportunity through that prism. On the other hand, if we view valuing diversity as a long-term culture change, we are likely to identify different obstacles and develop a very different set of recommendations for change. While one may be tempted to go for a quick resolution, this is not likely to produce sustainable change. To reap the benefits of this innovation, we must appreciate that it is not a program but an exciting new paradigm. Then we must approach it with a broad and penetrating perspective because, in the end, our own expectations will in large part shape the future reality of this effort.

FIVE

Understanding the Change Process

I t is no overstatement to say that understanding the dynamics of change is essential to the successful implementation of all valuing diversity efforts. Yet, sadly, few organizations have applied proven change adoption principles to diversity implementation. As a result, the fundamental paradigm shift required for full adoption of this new concept has been unnecessarily delayed.

This is particularly ironic since change management is not an unfamiliar concept in most organizations where diversity implementation has already begun. Because accelerated change has become an integral part of organization life, change management is now a familiar topic at executive board meetings, management seminars, and virtually everywhere people meet to plan an organization's future.

While the theories vary slightly, one underlying message is found in all popular change models: *Within every organization, people respond to new ideas in distinct and predictable ways, based on differences in individual tolerance of perceived risk.* This tolerance runs the gamut from active search for new ideas and uncritical acceptance of innovation through suspicion, and a wait-and-see reluctance to adopt change, to the extreme of unthinking, even hostile rejection of change. The variations in this individual response to new ideas have been categorized by behavioral scientists into five distinct response groups, each group either more or less tolerant of change than the others.

In the behavioral science field, where research on change adoption abounds, thousands of studies have been conducted documenting these classic human responses to change.[1] Whenever people in organizations are asked to endorse or adopt new ideas, such patterned responses occur. Needless to say, understanding these classic patterns can be extremely helpful in diversity implementation planning.

But while change adoption research has been used in many companies to help market new products and services, it is seldom referenced in designing and implementing diversity initiatives. Despite their time-tested reliability and practical value in introducing and accelerating acceptance of new ideas (from birth control pills to new agricultural methods), change adoption principles have been virtually overlooked by most diversity specialists and managers. Nonetheless, applying these principles can greatly accelerate acceptance of

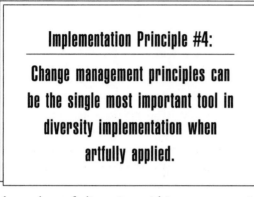

Implementation Principle #4:

Change management principles can be the single most important tool in diversity implementation when artfully applied.

the value of diversity within any organization; in fact, it is not an overstatement to say that change management principles can be the single most important tool in diversity implementation when artfully applied.

But if these principles are so effective, why aren't they in wide use now in organizations implementing diversity? One reason is that many managers and diversity specialists still think of diversity implementation in training terms only. They do not yet see it as systemic culture change; therefore, they have not made use of the tools available to help manage and accelerate system change. In addition, some organizations still believe the EEO/AA mandated approach to change is the way to implement diversity. Using this method, you simply tell managers whom to hire and promote, as well as how many and how fast, and you are done. Hopefully, if you were not already convinced, Chapter 3 has persuaded you that this is definitely not the most effective method of accelerating acceptance of diversity.

Finally, there are people who resist using any type of predictive model to anticipate reactions within a group, believing that such models stereotype individuals. But can a model stereotype people, or do people behave in somewhat predictable ways when faced with uncertainty and change? Not using change adoption principles to plan diversity implementation is like walking on a well-marked forest trail—and refusing to read the signs. While you may eventually get to where you want to go without these aids, you are also much more likely to get lost along the way.

Understanding how groups respond to change doesn't pigeonhole people; on the contrary, it can help people climb out of their pigeonholes. This knowledge gives us a more accurate, less subjective way of interpreting patterns in group behavior and successfully modifying that behavior. Pretending that behavior patterns do not exist does not cause them to go away. It simply keeps us in a perpetual state of mystification regarding the ways in which people react to change.

Because valuing diversity is an innovation that challenges the old order, understanding how this change is likely to be adopted and resisted in an organization is crucial in implementation planning. Without this perspective, those who guide diversity implementation are likely to increase the time required to institutionalize this change. They are also likely to become frustrated and create frustration throughout the organization as they proceed down the path. Ultimately, they can fail in their efforts to change the culture if they ignore the classic response patterns to change or attempt to work against the tide of human nature.

Change Adoption and Valuing Diversity

When an innovation or change like valuing diversity is introduced into an organization, managers and employees don't all immediately want to adopt it. Instead, this change is typically greeted with enthusiasm by some, skepticism by many and even hostility by a few. Like any new idea, valuing diversity moves through an organization, gaining momentum and support in a predictable pattern. In the early stages of introduction, diversity will be adopted by a small group of idealistic, committed people. Later on after the trial and error stage is over and there are successful results to point to among the early adopters, the majority of people will begin to buy in. Eventually, if implementation is successful, valuing diversity will become part of the mainstream culture with just a few laggards left to continue resisting it.

While there is always a small group ahead of the curve when it comes to accepting a new idea, most people will only adopt the value of diversity after satisfying themselves that this change is not just a fad. They will first want to be certain that the change will not harm them and that it will lead to favorable results. In deciding whether or not to buy in, they will want to know how diversity will impact their work groups. Some will require bottom-line evidence that valuing diversity makes good financial sense. Others will require assurances that the boss really supports this change before they adopt it. As with any new idea, there will also be a small segment of the organization that never buys in—or is only willing to accept this change after valuing diversity is thoroughly institutionalized in the organization.

Perceived Risks

Why do some people spark to the idea of valuing diversity and others do not? This variety in response occurs because of differences in the ratio of opportunity to risk that people perceive when asked to value diversity. Some individuals perceive greater risk in embracing the value of diversity than do others. This perception may be due to a generally high level of discomfort with change itself—a personality trait. It may be due to a lack of firsthand knowledge and experience with diversity—not knowing enough about other cultures to make an informed decision to value diversity. It may also be that an individual's perception of risk is based upon social conditioning. The more biased and ingrained one's belief system is against cultural diversity, the greater one's perception of risk is likely to be.

And just what are the risks that people fear? Generally, the perceived risks fall into two categories: performance-based risk and image-based risk. In the case of perceived performance risk, people question: Will diversity add value? Will this new paradigm work as well as the traditional one we're more accustomed to? Is something liable to go wrong? How can I be sure, despite what the experts say, that valuing diversity will live up to its promise and enhance teamwork and innovation? Will accepting diversity make my life happier, more rewarding, and more secure, or will it do the opposite?

In the case of image-based risk, a different set of underlying questions is often asked: Will I look foolish for embracing this idea if other knowledgeable people reject it? Will I be perceived as radical? too liberal? not bottom-line driven? Will I ultimately be rejected by my friends and colleagues? There may also be a strong, underlying concern: I might fail by association if I support this idea. If I value diversity, I may lose and others may gain.

Diversity Adoption Curve

Based on extensive behavioral science research examining how innovations move through many different types of organizations, the Diversity Adoption Curve that follows depicts the typical flow or path that valuing diversity takes as it is introduced and adopted within an organization. Like a wave forming and rolling toward the shore, valuing diversity is initially embraced by a small, select group of innovators in an organization. As this new paradigm gains momentum, it is then embraced by the change agents, who speed up the wave and accelerate its movement through the organization. Slowly, after a period of successful testing and refinement, the wave gathers the strength required to become a change that the majority of people in an organization begin to accept. Ultimately, it will dash itself powerfully upon the rocks of the last resistant segment of the population and begin wearing away their hostility and gaining acceptance among those most opposed from the start.

We do not create this wave of new-idea adoption. This is simply the way the sea of innovation functions, whether we recognize the pattern or not, whether we influence it or not. Our opportunity lies in speeding up this natural, ubiquitous process that leads to desirable change: making diversity a valued asset more quickly and more thoroughly. Our opportunity as implementers of change lies in using this understanding of why people resist and accept new ideas to make the process of change more efficient, more certain, and more effective.

All members of an organization fall into one of the five segments shown on the Diversity Adoption Curve. Within each distinct segment, people share certain attitudes and assumptions about the value of diversity. The five segments include:

- Innovators
- Change agents
- Pragmatists
- Skeptics
- Traditionalists

The Diversity Adoption Process

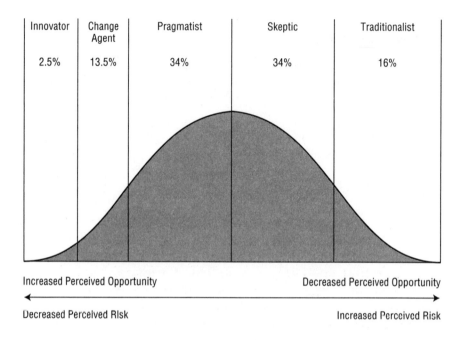

Innovator	Change Agent	Pragmatist	Skeptic	Traditionalist
2.5%	13.5%	34%	34%	16%

Increased Perceived Opportunity   Decreased Perceived Opportunity

◄—————————————————————————————————————►

Decreased Perceived Risk   Increased Perceived Risk

According to the Diversity Adoption Curve, one's placement in a particular segment is based on the level of perceived opportunity and risk associated with valuing diversity. For example, as an innovator my view of valuing diversity would be likely to focus much more on the opportunities that it offers while believing I can readily handle any potential risks. In contrast, moving to the right side of the curve, as a skeptic I would be more inclined to view valuing diversity as a potential threat to my security and disruption of my comfortable and familiar attitudes and practices. The farther to the left of the curve, the more likely it is that we perceive valuing diversity as an opportunity. The farther to the right, the more likely it is that we fear this change and perceive it as a threat.

It is important to note that the bell curve depicted above delineates how groups typically respond to *any* promising new idea.

To illustrate this point, let us consider dancing as an example. While few people (innovators) actually invent new dances, some people (change agents) watch the innovators and occasionally adopt a step that looks interesting to them. Until they see a good dancer using this step, most people (pragmatists) wouldn't think of trying it in public, and some (skeptics) will not try it until the majority of people on the dance floor are doing it. Finally, there are those people (traditionalists) who will say, "Why change? If the two-step was good enough for my grandad, it's still good enough for me!"

In study after study of real-life situations in a variety of organizations, adoption or full acceptance of innovation among individuals replicates this curve. Therefore, one can anticipate that in any company, government agency, law firm, university, and so on, *where diversity implementation occurs, this curve will represent the predictable pattern of adoption that will occur among employees.* As such, given a moderate expectation or promise of gain, the percentage of total population shown in each segment of the Diversity Adoption Curve will be generally consistent across all organizations for all reasonable innovations.

Variables Affecting Adoption

While the general pattern of the movement of change through a population stays the same, there are several variables that affect the relative speed of adoption, causing some changes to be adopted quickly and others more slowly. These variables have more to do with perception than with reality. Therefore, they influence the speed of change adoption, even if they are factors only in the eye of the potential adopter and not hard objective facts.

The following table contrasts characteristics that speed innovation with those that slow it down:

Speeds up adoption	Slows down adoption
Compatibility	Incompatibility
Simplicity	Complexity
Testability	Little/No testability
Observability	Little/No observability
High relative advantage	Little/No relative advantage

Key Questions:

In assessing each of the variables, consider the current environment in your organization and ask yourself the following questions:

Compatibility:
How similar is valuing diversity to present attitudes, beliefs, and practices in your organization?

Simplicity:
How simple is it to understand valuing diversity and to implement the idea?

Testability:
Can the idea be tested in a small segment of the organization first? Can successes be easily replicated in other departments or work groups?

Observability:
When diversity is valued, can people in the company easily see the results?

Relative Advantage:
How great an improvement will valuing diversity make in your organization when compared to the traditional practices it is expected to replace?

Where does valuing diversity generally stand when these characteristics are used to assess its probable speed of adoption? While answers will vary somewhat from company to company, this change generally lacks at least three of the perceived characteristics that speed adoption: compatibility, simplicity, and observability.

Because it is a new paradigm, valuing diversity invariably challenges some existing assumptions, beliefs, and practices in an organization; therefore, it is often not perceived as highly compatible with the organizational status quo. In fact, many changes are required to embed this value in a company.

While it is a simple concept to understand, valuing diversity is not easily put into practice. Lack of knowledge about other cultures and unconscious biases often interfere with implementation of this philosophy. The time and effort required to overcome these problems also discourages many people from embarking on the path to greater knowledge. Finally, when diversity is being valued, it is not something that is always observable. One must look at patterns in turnover, productivity, sales, and innovation over time to "see" the positive results of implementing diversity.

Fortunately, in many organizations valuing diversity scores much higher on perceived testability and relative advantage. Regardless of relative size or complexity, pilot projects that demonstrate improvements in productivity, customer satisfaction, innovation, employee retention, and demographic profile are highly feasible in every organization. Yet, few companies are taking the time to conduct such small-scale change efforts. Instead, those that move beyond training are opting for widescale implementation of change as a first step. This decision has serious implications for the long-term viability of culture change that will be explored further in Chapter 6.

Finally, positive perceptions about the relative advantages of this change can also be readily communicated and reinforced. When organizations share internal data highlighting the costs in dollars and human capital of not valuing diversity, they are acknowledging the need for change. This acknowledgment adds ballast to the case for valuing diversity. Workforce demographics and globalization of markets also contribute to building a case for this change. In addition, as companies create internal success stories through small-scale change efforts and pilot programs, they also impact employee perceptions of relative advantage.

In developing an implementation plan for valuing diversity, one must begin with a solid change management framework. The Diversity Adoption Curve is a sound framework for understanding how people react to and resist change. Unlike other models that offer minimal guidance, this model points to five distinct subgroups that exist in every organization and perceive change differently. By understanding the unique motivational and informational needs of innovators, change agents, pragmatists, skeptics, and traditionalists, we can tailor communications, education, and systems changes to better meet their needs. In doing so, we increase the probability that valuing diversity will ultimately be adopted by every segment.

By understanding the perceived characteristics that can speed adoption of change, we also can build support among employees by emphasizing the testability and relative advantage that diversity offers at the start of implementation. At the same time, we must be realistic about the perceptual barriers that exist and recognize that this new paradigm will present us with many challenges on the journey to full adoption.

Valuing diversity is a deep and fundamental change. Although simple to understand, it is not easy to put into practice. While it offers important long-term benefits to individuals and organizations, these benefits are not always tangible or easily seen. To speed adoption, the issues surrounding compatibility, complexity, and observability must all be addressed. In Chapter 6, we will explore the distinct worlds of innovators, change agents, pragmatists, skeptics, and traditionalists in order to fully address these concerns.

SIX

Profiling the Organization

I ronically, the principle of change adoption or movement of a new idea through a series of increasingly resistant groups is a model that is itself initially resisted by pragmatists and opposed by skeptics and traditionalists. As such, the "proof of the pudding" is in the resistance to its eating! While this book is less likely to appeal to segments lower on the adoption curve, if you find yourself resisting this change model, I encourage you to read on as we build the practical, business-based case for using the adoption curve to implement diversity.

Segment Characteristics[1]

Based upon research and experience, we know that everyone in an organization will not adopt the value of diversity at the same time. We also know that everyone will not initially view diversity as an opportunity. Instead, there will be increasing levels of resistance to this change in each segment of the employee population from innovators (the least resistant) through change agents, pragmatists, and skeptics to traditionalists (the most resistant).

In addition to using the diversity adoption curve to plan implementation, *there are also five distinct profiles for innovators, change agents, pragmatists, skeptics, and traditionalists that outline the distinct assumptions, motivations, and needs of each group.* These profiles are based on the results of extensive change adoption research pertaining to the introduction and acceptance of hundreds of new ideas, products, and services in many organizations and among diverse, multicultural populations.

The following is a brief description of each segment as represented in the Diversity Adoption Curve. As we discussed in Chapter 5, individuals within a segment share a particular set of assumptions and expectations about valuing diversity. No two segments see the

47

risks or opportunities associated with this change in exactly the same way. Each segment also requires different types of information in order to be persuaded to adopt the value of diversity. Finally, the speed of adoption varies dramatically across the five segments. As you read through the descriptions, think about yourself and the people with whom you work. Ask yourself, Which segment most accurately describes my attitudes and beliefs about valuing diversity? Which segment(s) best describe my colleagues' opinions and beliefs? How do I and my colleagues react to other changes in the work environment (e.g., new procedures, technologies, structures, people, or other changing requirements)?

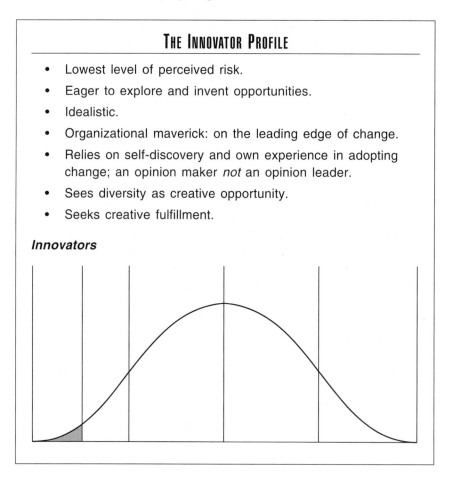

THE INNOVATOR PROFILE

- Lowest level of perceived risk.
- Eager to explore and invent opportunities.
- Idealistic.
- Organizational maverick: on the leading edge of change.
- Relies on self-discovery and own experience in adopting change; an opinion maker *not* an opinion leader.
- Sees diversity as creative opportunity.
- Seeks creative fulfillment.

Innovators

In every organization, there is a small group of individuals (approximately 2.5 percent) that seems to quietly embrace new ideas long before others recognize their value. These are the **innovators.** Members of this group are likely to see valuing diversity as a creative opportunity. They are idealistic about its positive potential and perceive much possible gain and little risk associated with this change.

Innovators are constantly seeking new ideas and methods. Valuing diversity is viewed as such a method by innovators. In fact, many may already be successfully managing and leveraging diversity within their own work groups when implementation is just beginning elsewhere in the organization.

As the organization becomes more focused on implementation, innovators may appear bored or impatient with the dialogue and debate that are necessary parts of the culture change process. This often occurs because they are farther down the path towards valuing diversity than most of their colleagues. While they have strong convictions about the value of diversity and the creative benefits it offers, innovators are not likely to engage in much public discussion about their commitment. Because they are not as socially interactive as change agents, they may be regarded by many as eccentric and even deviant. The reason is that innovators often operate outside the established norms of the mainstream organization in their search for creative solutions to complex problems. Because they tend to operate outside the mainstream, innovators prefer to practice valuing diversity rather than preach to others about it. As such, they can be considered opinion makers, not opinion leaders.

Although they recognize the importance of culture change, innovators will be likely to support implementation from a distance rather than take an interactive leadership role in the change process. Because they rely on their own knowledge and experience when it comes to diversity adoption, they often may not be interested in corporate seminars and awareness training aimed at speeding adoption. Instead, they seek out whatever knowledge they need to make diversity work without relying on the organization to provide the rationale for this change or the information required to successfully implement diversity.

THE CHANGE AGENT PROFILE

- Low level of perceived risk in change.
- Interested in exploring opportunities/issues.
- Optimistic and an early tester of new ideas.
- Likes to influence implementation and lead change.
- Seeks out and passes on information; an opinion leader.
- Sees diversity as knowledge-enhancing and good for people.
- Seeks recognition, respect, social leadership, and personal fulfillment.

Change Agents

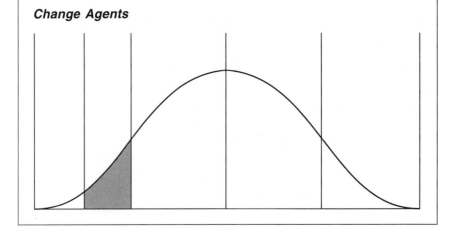

Unlike the innovators, who prefer to work behind the scenes, **change agents** want to be out front and visible in their support for new and better ideas. They are the true opinion leaders in building support for valuing diversity and enjoy being recognized by others in the organization for playing a proactive, visible role. Change agents are social people. They tend to be "tuned up" to the underlying needs and desires of others in their organization. As such, they are attracted to valuing diversity because they believe it is good for people.

Particularly in the early stages of implementation, change agents welcome information about diversity issues and opportunities just as a singer welcomes new songs or an artist welcomes a palette of vibrant paints. Personal knowledge enhancement is a strong motivator for change agents. They will participate in seminars, read books, rent films, and engage in frequent dialogue with diverse people in order to understand more about the complexity of the issues and their impact on different groups. As they build a broad knowledge base and acquire personal experience, change agents also like to pass on their learnings to others in the organization. Because of their desire for social interaction, they can be important conduits in communicating about diversity with groups farther to their right on the Diversity Adoption Curve.

While innovators will adopt the value of diversity earlier than change agents, their adoption will not necessarily motivate the rest of the organization to follow. Because they work behind the scenes and are often regarded as eccentrics, innovators' actions do not shape corporate opinion to a great degree. However, their actions do attract the attention of change agents who tend to "look over the innovators' shoulders" in order to find new ideas that appear particularly useful.

By selectively supporting the most practical and valuable ideas of the innovators, the change agents shape mass opinion. Once they are convinced that valuing diversity offers some benefit both personally and to others, change agents will become actively involved in facilitating broader acceptance of this change throughout the organization. As knowledgeable supporters of the value of diversity, they are powerful opinion leaders. Not only do they provide social sanction for many of the innovator's ideas, but because they are socially interactive and well networked, change agents can also be very influential in convincing their more skeptical colleagues to support the value of diversity.

Change agents are optimistic about potential opportunity—the kind of opportunity that valuing diversity offers. Because they desire the social benefits of this change, such as increased cooperation, mutual respect, and recognition as a leader, change agents are eager to spread the word and encourage others to become more engaged. If there is a call for pilot participants, facilitators, mentors, role models, or people to give testimony about the value of diversity during implementation, the change agents will be the first to volunteer. Generally, this group represents about 13.5 percent of the total organization.

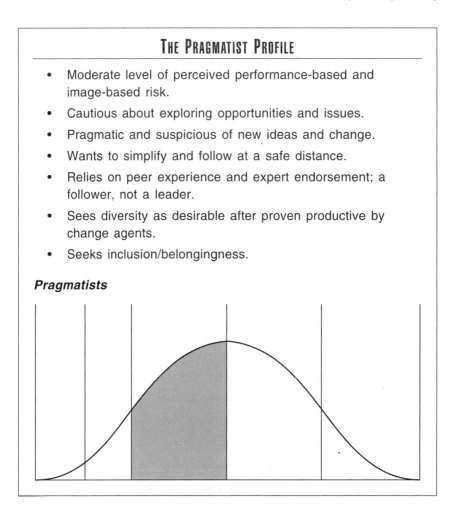

THE PRAGMATIST PROFILE

- Moderate level of perceived performance-based and image-based risk.
- Cautious about exploring opportunities and issues.
- Pragmatic and suspicious of new ideas and change.
- Wants to simplify and follow at a safe distance.
- Relies on peer experience and expert endorsement; a follower, not a leader.
- Sees diversity as desirable after proven productive by change agents.
- Seeks inclusion/belongingness.

Pragmatists

If one could choose just two words to capture the general attitude that **pragmatists** have about valuing diversity, those words would have to be "Show me." Unlike the two groups already discussed, pragmatists are neither creatively idealistic nor particularly humanistic or socially motivated when it comes to valuing diversity. They are not moved by moral arguments. They don't necessarily regard valuing diversity as the right thing to do. Instead, it is the simple, straight-forward, practical, bottom-line consequences of valuing diversity that appeal most to this group.

Pragmatists are suspicious of change. They are people who perceive the glass to be half empty and are more concerned with potential loss than potential gain. Because they see a moderate amount of performance-based risk associated with adopting the value of diversity, they are reluctant to move quickly towards embracing it. They want to be convinced first that there is a solid business case. They want to see live examples of diversity in action within their own organization. Pragmatists won't seriously consider adoption until they see how their change agent colleagues fare in managing this innovation. They also want reassurance from experts that this change is a safe one to make before they will risk their professional standing and consider adopting it.

Pragmatists, who make up approximately 34 percent of an organization, rely on the experiences of colleagues and endorsements of experts to influence and guide their decisions about valuing diversity. Pragmatists often find internal success stories involving trusted colleagues to be the most convincing arguments for adoption of change. Because they want to be accepted by their more innovative peers, pragmatists eventually do adopt change but are likely to take many months or even years longer to decide. Since they are a very large segment of every organization, pragmatists are an important group to focus on during implementation. Interfacing them with change agents, who have success stories to tell about the benefits of valuing diversity, is one important way to speed their adoption.

THE SKEPTIC PROFILE

- High level of perceived performance and image-based risk.
- Closed to personal exploration of opportunities and fearful of issues.
- Skeptical about new ideas.
- Mainstream popularity is required before she or he will try.
- Relies heavily on authority and majority endorsements.
- Sees diversity as potentially harmful and moving too fast.
- Seeks security and wide endorsement by the mainstream.

(continued)

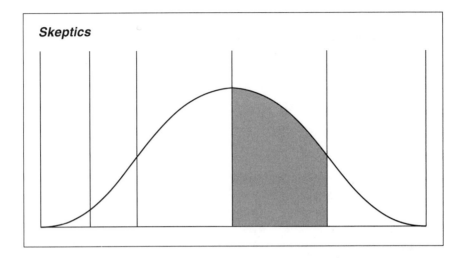

Skeptics

As we move farther to the left on the curve, we find another large segment (about 34 percent of the organization) that perceives a high degree of risk associated with change and innovation. These are the **skeptics.** Unlike the pragmatists, who want compelling business reasons for valuing diversity, this group is likely to start out suspicious of any case made for diversity—even the strategic business case. Skeptics are very slow to adopt the value of diversity. Because they fear it will fail, they want to protect their image and avoid association with this change. They may even seek out negative examples of situations where diversity did not work in the organization as a means of slowing implementation and maintaining the status quo.

Communications aimed at influencing skeptics to value diversity must first pass through the varied filters of these reluctant receivers. Unless messages are carefully and skillfully crafted, skeptics are liable to overlook, ignore, distort, and argue with those that support the value of diversity. Similarly, training and education are also filtered through the skeptics' screens of selective perception, attention, retention, and action. The following chart[2] illustrates how the impact of communication and training are minimized as ideas are filtered out and/or distorted along the way:

Total Audience			Just . . .
Selective exposure	Those who read and listen		**look . . .**
Selective perception	Those who hear without distortion		**how . . .**
Selective retention	Those who internalize and remember		**it . . .**
Selective action	Those who act based on training and communication	**drops!**	

Even after pragmatists buy into the importance of valuing diversity, skeptics will still be questioning the need for change. As communication and training increase, many will assert that change is moving too fast. To adopt any new idea or change, skeptics require a strong, convincing endorsement from their leaders. Once they are convinced that those in positions of authority, as well as the majority of their peers, are behind this change, they will then bow to hierarchic and social pressure and begin to accept the new paradigm.

Because they fear change, skeptics are not willing to invest their time or energies to work for culture change. On the contrary, since they perceive significant risks associated with valuing diversity, skeptics will work to slow down the change process by ignoring and distorting reality. Only after diversity has achieved wide mainstream acceptance will this group seriously consider adoption.

Given their reluctance to support change, skeptics can create conflict in organizations and stir sympathy among pragmatists if they are coerced into supporting diversity efforts or punished for expressing their concerns. Because they are a large segment of the organization, skeptics can create a powerful backlash that can ultimately defeat the change process. To avoid this backlash and build momentum for change, it is important to take skeptics' fears into account when planning communications, training, and systems change. Like the horse that can be drawn to water but not forced to drink, skeptics are ultimately convinced by time and mainstream support for the value of diversity to adopt this change, not by a baseball bat to the head or a forceful push from behind. Although the latter may be tempting strategies, they are likely to push skeptics deeper into denial and resistance and consequently move the change process backwards instead of forwards.

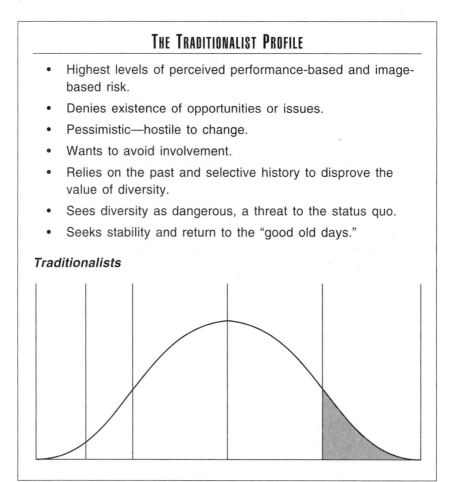

THE TRADITIONALIST PROFILE

- Highest levels of perceived performance-based and image-based risk.
- Denies existence of opportunities or issues.
- Pessimistic—hostile to change.
- Wants to avoid involvement.
- Relies on the past and selective history to disprove the value of diversity.
- Sees diversity as dangerous, a threat to the status quo.
- Seeks stability and return to the "good old days."

Traditionalists

As we move farther to the right, we find the group that is slowest to adopt change—the **traditionalists.** This group associates the highest levels of both performance-based risk and image-based risk with adoption of the value of diversity. As such, traditionalists will work to halt culture change and will often distort reality to derail the change adoption process.

Unlike the innovators who are focused on the future, traditionalists are focused on the past. Their decisions about valuing diversity are likely to be influenced by their selective remembrances of better days gone by. Traditionalists will often deny the existence of opportunities and real issues associated with valuing diversity. They will distort issues to satisfy their need for continuity with the past. This denial/distortion process helps traditionalists avoid engaging change.

Traditionalists, who comprise about 16 percent of an organization, tend to be fearful, pessimistic, and even hostile about valuing diversity. They try to avoid this change as long as it is possible to do so. Most yearn for a return to the good old days, believing that they themselves and their organizations were better off before valuing diversity came along. Some traditionalists never accept the new paradigm. Others support diversity only after the organization institutionalizes this change, making it the standard by which all performance is measured. Once valuing diversity becomes the institutional standard, traditionalists will begin to accept it, fearing that they will be penalized by the organization if they do not.

When the fear of negative consequences associated with not valuing diversity outweighs the fear of diversity itself, adoption is most likely to begin occurring in this group; however, it is typical for traditionalists to lag behind the rest of the organization by several years on the path to change. In some cases, adoption by traditionalists simply never occurs. Instead, some may decide to leave the organization once valuing diversity becomes the new reality and can no longer be avoided.

While traditionalists can be very innovative on other issues, they may buy state-of-the art computers, wear their baseball caps back-to-front, or enjoy the latest clothing styles—the personal risk that they associate with valuing diversity makes it difficult for them to evolve beyond this segment on this issue. Although some may move up the curve and become skeptics, the majority will remain in this group, seeking security in the status quo and avoiding change whenever possible.

Benefits of Resistance

Given the comments made about resistance thus far in this chapter, one might conclude that all resistance to change is counterproductive. But this is not always the case. In some instances, resistance among employees can help organizations maintain stability in periods of rapid change. It can also help them separate practical, beneficial ideas from the fads and the gimmicks. Because they are suspicious of innovation, skeptics and traditionalists can prevent organizations from pursuing ideas that appear reasonable on the surface but, on closer examination, are seriously flawed—the strap-on-the-wings, jump-from-the-Eiffel-Tower, and flap-your-arms-on-the-way-down type of idea.

Skeptics and traditionalists are an organization's anchor to windward. They demand testing over time and a reasoned process for assessing results in order to arrive at relatively risk-free solutions. Their cautious approach to adopting change forces others to their left on the Diversity Adoption Curve to build a stronger case—one that minimizes risk as it maximizes potential. In addition, the skeptics and traditionalists give longevity to ideas that they finally adopt, since they will not abandon them any more quickly than they accepted them.

Although it may be uncomfortable to acknowledge differences in openness to change that exist across segments, we are far less likely to institutionalize the value of diversity if we ignore the differences or deny their existence. Regardless of how we want them to behave and feel, skeptics and traditionalists are very negative about change. If this were not the case, then valuing diversity and all other promising ideas would be readily accepted in organizations. Unfortunately, the reality is that this paradigm has yet to be fully adopted in any organization and, in some cases, seems to be losing rather than gaining support over time. One principal reason for this lagging momentum is the one-size-fits-all approach used in many organizations to prepare people for this change.

Diverse Segments Require Diverse Strategies

Because the amount of time and the types of information needed to win support for change differ among innovators, change agents, pragmatists, skeptics, and traditionalists, a single, uniform approach to implementing diversity and uniform timing will not be equally effective across all segments. For example, while diversity as the right thing to do will be a persuasive argument among innovators and change agents, it will not create momentum for adoption within the other segments.

To assure that diversity implementation is as rapid and successful as possible, the different needs and concerns of all five segments on the Diversity Adoption Curve must be factored into the overall plan. Each segment should be targeted for focused, specific attention over time. Then, a staged approach to communication, education, and change implementation must be designed to reduce levels of perceived risk and systematically build the momentum and support required for full adoption.

> ## Implementation Principle #5:
>
> To assure that diversity implementation is as rapid and successful as possible, the different needs and concerns of all five segments on the Diversity Adoption Curve must be factored into the overall plan.

If our goal is to build support for the value of diversity, we must be strategic in our approach. First, we must profile the organization using the Diversity Adoption Curve. Who are the innovators? Where are the change agents and pragmatists? These three groups should be identified at the outset before implementation begins. Some change agents will self-identify, volunteering to get involved early in the process. Categorization of the innovators and pragmatists may require more formal screening methods, such as interviews, self-assessment questionnaires, and feedback from employee-opinion surveys.

Once the organization is profiled and we have identified the three segments most open to change, we must enlist the help and energies of innovators and change agents to make ready the environment. As we proceed, we must be careful to involve those segments further to the right on the Diversity Adoption Curve only in activities that will reduce their perceptions of risk and not increase them. At every decision point, we must ask ourselves: Will a one-size-fits-all approach to education, communications, and so on, really work, or do we need to modify our programs and our timing to reach or target diverse segments?

While diversity in implementation occurs today in some organizations, it often happens more by accident than because of systematic planning. In the interest of accelerating adoption of the value of diversity and minimizing backlash, *it is time to apply the Diversity Adoption Curve to implementation planning in every organization.* By using it, we can ensure that adoption of the value of diversity happens more quickly, systematically, and painlessly. By ignoring this useful tool, we simply increase our own risk of getting lost along the way or of having the wrong idea adopted—that diversity has a negative value. For the point has often been made that in every attempt at desirable change there is a sale made. Either you sell *your* idea or they sell *theirs*!

SEVEN

Acquiring the Diversity Mindset

As we now know, both defining diversity and distinguishing it from EEO/AA are important steps in the early stages of change implementation. Approaching this change as a paradigm shift that requires a redefinition of related problems and opportunities is another critical step in facilitating this change. While it would seem that taking these steps should ensure success for diversity implementation, this is not the case; for knowledge alone is not enough. To successfully facilitate change, there is one more critical requirement: the diversity mindset.

While not easily categorized, this mindset is what separates effective diversity facilitators and managers from those who play at or pay lip service to the need for change. The valuing diversity mindset functions as an internal regulator, keeping our beliefs and actions consistent. It engages both our heads and hearts in promoting culture change. It gives us the compassion required to understand others' needs and fears, the courage to face conflict and opposition, and the conceptual grounding to develop creative solutions to complex organizational problems.

> ## Implementation Principle #6:
>
> The diversity mindset is what separates effective facilitators and managers from those who play at or pay lip service to the need for change.

This mindset also gives us the ethical commitment required to make appropriate choices and to consistently do the right things for the right reasons. It lifts our spirits when we face frustration and, like a helpful guide, keeps us on the path.

Unlike many change management skills that can be quickly learned and applied, the valuing diversity mindset is an attitudinal state that can only be achieved through lifelong learning, personal investment, and continuous self-improvement. While we may recognize this mindset when observing others who put it into practice, we cannot simply mimic what we see. Instead, we must first accept and internalize four basic beliefs. These beliefs form the foundation of the valuing diversity mindset and include the following:

Belief #1: Valuing diversity requires long-term culture change.

Belief #2: Valuing diversity is good for people and good for business.

Belief #3: Valuing diversity implementation must be inclusive, not exclusive.

Belief #4: Valuing diversity benefits everyone.

Long-Term Culture Change

How long does it take to change a culture? So far, experience with diversity implementation in many organizations would suggest that the answer is "much longer than we initially think." In many respects, the valuing diversity paradigm challenges attitudes and assumptions that have built up over decades and have been passed down through generations. These attitudes are not likely to be modified overnight. Because this paradigm is a deep, fundamental change for most people and for every organization, facilitating implementation is challenging and requires time. Valuing diversity is neither easily understood nor readily adopted in organizations. Even after it becomes a widely accepted goal, it is still not readily put into practice by most individuals.

Valuing diversity can be a source of discomfort for many individuals when first introduced in an organization. This is because it is a paradigm that challenges individual and organizational biases about core identity, values, and how we interact with each other.

In most organizations, there is a high degree of emotionality sur-rounding diversity implementation. Sometimes feelings expressed by those who are more resistant to this change may create concern and doubt among the strongest supporters of diversity. These supporters may question whether change is really possible. What helps people through these inevitable moments of doubt is a valuing diversity mindset.

This mindset allows us to see the long-term benefits that will be achieved when diversity is truly valued in the organization. By keeping this long-term vision in focus, we can help others see the benefits as well. Our confidence that the organization is on the right path can increase the confidence that others have in the positive potential of this change. Knowing that valuing diversity is a deep and broad culture change also helps us remember that full adoption will not occur in a few months. Instead, organizational buy-in is likely to take several years, a decade, or perhaps even longer.

Unlike the larger U.S. society, where most neighborhoods and communities remain divided along racial, ethnic, and income lines, the workplace of the 1990s is a multicultural environment in most organizations. It is the arena where diverse groups routinely come together to engage in collective enterprise. As such, it is the place where the need for mutual respect, cooperation, and trust that transcends cultural differences is most evident.

In many respects then, valuing diversity in organizations ad-dresses issues that our larger society is not addressing. It is a culture change that encourages people to look deeper and to find value where they have seldom seen it before. It challenges each of us to demonstrate respect, cooperation, and cultural sensitivity in our interactions with others. In effect, it is asking people to adopt a change that U.S. society has yet to embrace.

Without the involvement and support of the larger society, valuing diversity is a more difficult change to bring about inside any organization. In order to be proactive and avoid cynicism in the early stages of implementation, people who facilitate this change must take a systemic, long-term view. Their mindsets must help them see valuing diversity as a comprehensive, long-term change process and not a program or isolated event.

Ethical/Business Benefits

Although some people are attracted to the value of diversity because of a strong belief that it is good for people, the majority of employees in an organization will not be. Instead, most will want basic bottom-line evidence of the need for this change. Therefore, those who want to facilitate change across the organization must recognize and emphasize the business benefits as well as the people benefits in order to reach the majority of people. Fortunately, this is not difficult to do.

While valuing diversity is good for people, it is business itself that stands to reap the greatest benefit from adopting this change. Whether management is aware of the costs or not, every organization pays a heavy price in reduced productivity, lost sales, limited innovation, higher absenteeism, and higher turnover when diversity is not valued. Although most businesses make little effort to measure these costs, the price is still high. When diversity is valued, there is greater innovation. There is also enhanced teamwork and mutual respect. All of these characteristics contribute to a positive work environment. Together, they make it easier for people from diverse backgrounds to join, to feel supported, and to contribute.

Businesses that value diversity also operate more comfortably and strategically in an increasingly diverse global marketplace. They are more skillful at appealing to diverse customer segments. They are more able to understand what diverse clients want. When a business sells a product or service comparable to others sold by competitors, valuing diversity can become the competitive advantage that wins new customers and builds loyalty among older ones.

Understanding that this change is good for people and for business enhances our ability as managers and diversity facilitators to influence others. By talking about the benefits of this change from two perspectives, we can reach more people. We can also seize more opportunities to leverage diversity in the global marketplace, simply because we see potential where others may not.

This dual perspective is like a set of glasses that allows us to look at situations from two different but related points of view. By developing a *people and business perspective,* we can challenge the old assumption that the interests of employees are in opposition to the interests of the organization; for when it comes to valuing diversity, this is simply not the case.

Inclusive versus Exclusive Process

Because the value and power of diversity lies in the ideas, experiences, and insights of people from every culturally diverse group, it is not possible to achieve full adoption while leaving any group(s) out. For diversity to be valued throughout an organization, all diverse groups must support the change implementation process. This support is more likely to occur once each group believes that its distinct voice is being heard by those facilitating this change. The following case history illustrates how important inclusion can be as a building block for change.

An Issue of "Readiness"

Mary Wilson is the diversity manager for a large power company. As the first person in the organization to be given this responsibility, she is eager to start the long process of culture change. Based on an initial climate survey that she conducted, Mary believes there is a serious glass ceiling above middle management for women and people of color throughout the company. Despite the fact that women comprise 39 percent of the total organization, there are none in senior management. Moreover, there are no African Americans or Hispanics in any operations management positions—the key line management jobs that tend to build careers.

Fearful that she will "spread her staff too thin" if she attempts to address other diversity issues that also surfaced, Mary has decided to make breaking the glass ceiling the group's priority for the next two years. Yesterday, she announced this plan to the senior executive staff and they supported her proposal.

This morning, Mary received a call from a white male manager who had heard about the glass ceiling initiative from his boss. He began the conversation by stating, "I was very upset when I heard about your plan. It doesn't go far enough. What about all the homophobic jokes that you hear around this place? Aren't you going to do anything to stop them?

"You know there isn't one gay person who feels safe enough to be out in this company. Can you imagine what would happen if I announced to the organization that I'm gay? My career would be over.

"I hate to say it, Mary, but this diversity plan seems rather elitist. You know there are a lot of other groups out there besides women and minorities in management who want to see things change. What are you going to do to help all our employees feel valued and respected?"

While Mary listens carefully to his comments, she is still convinced that her approach is correct. As far as homophobia is concerned, she explains that there is a "readiness issue" in the organization. While she agrees that more needs to be done to address the problem, she does not want to "overload the organization or push too hard at this point." The caller reacts to her comments by saying, "Readiness my foot! You sound like every other person I know who's afraid to deal with homophobia!"

Mary ends the conversation assuring the manager that she "hears his concerns" and will follow up with him soon. Afterwards, as she reflects on what happened, she realizes that the caller caught her by surprise. She was not prepared for the anger that he expressed. In replaying his comments, Mary concludes, "He has to understand that this initiative can't be all things to all people."

Although she would not admit it to anyone, Mary is also annoyed about the caller's comments. "Why can't the gays just wait their turn?" she muses. "After all, women and minorities have been fighting for equality a lot longer."

Key Questions:

1. Whose arguments are you more in agreement with, Mary's or the caller's?

2. Is Mary likely to facilitate this change successfully? Does she appear to have the valuing diversity mindset?

3. What might be done to make this implementation effort more inclusive?

4. Is your own organization's valuing diversity initiative inclusive? If not, which constituencies are being ignored or underrepresented?

5. What can be done to make it more inclusive?

Because enlightened self-interest is a primary reason for adopting the value of diversity, our self-interests as managers and facilitators of change can often affect the priorities we set during the initial stages of implementation. While we want to be inclusive, we may advocate more strongly for changes that directly impact us and groups to which we belong and less strongly for others. Yet it is this selective view of diversity's value and the presumption that "some people count more than others," that we are working as facilitators to challenge and change in the organization!

Assuming that most people will uncover more diversity issues and needs than they have time or resources to deal with, how can managers and diversity facilitators set priorities that have high impact without discounting anyone's "burning issue"? This delicate balance can best be achieved by adopting a wholistic view of diversity issues rather than a selective view. This wholistic view argues for creating an environment that respects all individuals and their diverse identities—not most or some or just a few.

A wholistic view of the issues helps us develop strategies and solutions that address the concerns of many diverse groups simultaneously. Rather than create a hierarchy of core dimensions to work on, we work to create an environment that values all of them. Rather than only address the needs of select groups, we work for changes that benefit all groups. Does this mean that mentoring programs for women or people of color would never be appropriate? Not necessarily. Instead, it means that such programs would first have to pass the inclusivity test. If special programs are developed for particular groups, what is being done for the remainder of the organization? How do such programs fit into the overall implementation plan? While diversity implementation can never be all things to all people, it must provide something for everyone in order to succeed.

Everyone Wins

Regardless of what core identities we each have, we all want to be happy, respected, and loved. In the workplace, we want to be recognized for who we are and appreciated for what we do. We want to feel comfortable with those with whom we work. We want to believe that our ideas and opinions are valued and that they influence important decisions that affect us and our work. These are basic desires that we all share, the common ground we stand on regardless of the differences in primary and secondary dimensions of diversity that separate us.

As managers and facilitators of culture change, we must be mindful of the fact that underneath all the issues surrounding diversity is a common set of human needs that unify us. Therefore, while we may describe our work in terms of enhancing productivity, innovation, and morale, we must also understand that it is about satisfying these basic needs in everyone. This is the true work of facilitating diversity culture change. Once we realize this, our ability to think wholistically about diversity and connect to people at a human level increases tenfold. As a result, culture change is no longer just possible, it becomes inevitable. For we cannot fail in our efforts to facilitate change if we make the interests of everyone in the organization our highest priority.

Unfortunately, the valuing diversity mindset is not yet a reality among managers and facilitators in every organization. Some people still do not recognize the need for long-term culture change or appreciate the importance of a wholistic, inclusive approach to diversity. As a result, many implementation efforts are stalled today or are not achieving their full potential. When we compare these stalled efforts, we see a consistent pattern of missteps along the way. In Section 2, we will explore some of the more common missteps that have occurred in organizations that are already implementing diversity. Hopefully, a careful analysis of these pitfalls will help some organizations move beyond these obstacles sooner or avoid them entirely as they introduce the diversity paradigm in the future.

TWO

Barriers to Implementation

EIGHT

Underinvesting and Overpromising

Whenever important changes are announced in an organization, employee expectations are immediately created. First, people want to understand how the changes will affect them personally. Then they what to know what overall impact these changes will have on their work groups and the operation. In keeping with this pattern, valuing diversity as a new paradigm for managing employees and serving customers also creates expectations when it is introduced. Among those who welcome this innovation, there is often a strong expectation that the organization will become more inclusive, open, and accepting of the contributions of employees from diverse cultural backgrounds. Among those who oppose this change, there is often a fearful expectation that increased emphasis on diversity will create instability and disrupt the status quo.

Valuing Diversity Raises Expectations

Because valuing diversity emphasizes inclusion and mutual respect, it is a change that gives hope to employees who may have felt marginalized or excluded in the past. When diversity initiatives are first introduced in an organization, it is not unusual for some employees to acknowledge that they are choosing to stay on in the hope that diversity will make a real difference. The promise of diversity is that powerful. But like any promise, an organization's follow-up actions must be consistent and strong if employees are to remain convinced that this culture change is real. This next case history illustrates what happens when an organization's promise is greater than its commitment to deliver.

THE LURE OF DIVERSITY

In 1988, this large, Midwestern law firm decided to begin an aggressive recruitment campaign to attract and hire attorneys of color for its nine offices throughout the United States. This decision to step up recruitment resulted after pressure was brought to bear on the firm to service particular client accounts with a racially diverse professional staff.

To head up this project, an African-American attorney, who had been with the firm for three years, was given full-time responsibility for associate recruitment and development. In his new role, he began visiting law schools and targeting students of color for summer internships. After a two-year nonstop networking effort, his perseverance began paying off. In 1990, the firm hired five African-American, two Mexican-American, and two Asian-American law students as interns.

During their summer internship, each of the eight students of color was given some exposure to the firm's four major practice groups. All were visited regularly by the firm's associate development director, who spoke of the "deep commitment to diversity in the firm" and the importance of "attorneys of color on the partner track." In addition, the group was wined and dined on a semi-monthly basis by several of the firm's senior partners.

The following year, eight of the nine students were offered, and accepted, full-time positions with the firm. Several mentioned the organization's commitment to diversity as one of the major reasons influencing their decisions to return full-time. Although most had been offered positions with more prestigious law firms, they still decided to go with this firm.

Since then, the eight associates of color hired in 1990 have all left the firm. Summing up what happened in the ensuing years, one explained, "The air turned pretty chilly once we were hired. During the next two years as we all looked up the career ladder, we couldn't help but notice that every other minority attorney hired before us failed to make partner. It was pretty demoralizing.

"Having a mentor relationship with a partner also seemed to be an important factor influencing advancement. Since none of us played golf at the country clubs where the partners did, we had no informal access. They didn't socialize with you if you didn't live in their part of town.

"When we got together and compared our experiences, it was also pretty clear that we were not getting any of the high-visibility 'plum' work assignments. So after two years every one of us started looking. After two more we were all gone. When I go to campuses now to recruit for my new firm and hear students talking about that firm's commitment to diversity, I feel very, very sad. They don't value diversity at all. They're just leading people on to make the numbers look better."

Key Questions:

1. Under what conditions is it ethical to use the "valuing diversity message" in recruiting to increase racial diversity?
2. When would it not be ethical to do so?
3. Once an effective recruitment strategy is in place, what else must an organization do to ensure high employee retention across all diverse groups?

Today, valuing diversity is becoming a competitive advantage in the employment marketplace. It is a reason that more people now cite for choosing one employer over another. Unfortunately, when an employer's rhetoric about valuing diversity far exceeds its action, employees can become cynical and demoralized. While the promise of diversity may attract some individuals to an organization, it will not convince them to stay there unless this initial promise is fulfilled with appropriate ongoing action.

Rhetoric versus Action

Beyond the rhetoric about diversity, it is the actions of managers towards employees and the interactions of co-workers at every level that tell the real valuing diversity story in an organization. Do they simply talk the talk or do they walk it? When companies are sincere about their commitment to valuing diversity, this sincerity is obvious. It is apparent in the policies that are employed to manage human resources and in the benefits that are offered. It is evident in the sensitive, ethical, and inclusive actions of senior managers. It is reflected in hiring and promotion patterns. Most of all, it is obvious in the comfort and enthusiasm displayed when people cross cultural lines to mentor, socialize, and get work accomplished. Ultimately, the ease and frequency of cross-cultural interaction among employees is the truest measure of whether this change is a mile wide and an inch deep or extends down into the fabric of the corporate culture.

As we know, creating an environment where all employees feel respected, included, and able to work together cooperatively is not easy. A long-term commitment to change is required. Unfortunately, while most businesses welcome the benefits that diversity brings, some are still not willing to make an investment in sustainable culture change. In such cases, the institutional gap between rhetoric and reality is very wide, and valuing diversity is often regarded as a "smoke and mirrors" attempt to lure a more diverse employee mix.

Fortunately, such misrepresentation is not likely to remain an effective recruiting strategy much longer. Job applicants today are digging below the surface to find out more about corporate diversity practices. They are asking for data to support corporate claims that diversity is valued. They are interviewing other employees, looking at demographic profiles, training, recognition and reward systems, corporate communications, and so on, and assessing the true level of organization commitment based on the facts rather than the rhetoric.

Corporate Commitment to Change

To truly benefit from interest in valuing diversity in the employment marketplace, companies must first decide if they are serious about institutionalizing this change. If their commitment extends beyond hiring to employee development, customer service, systems alignment, and culture change, then they are more likely to retain the employees and customers whom they attract with the valuing diversity message. If their commitment is superficial and based on potential short-term gain, then they would be well advised to abandon the diversity theme now; for there is no surer way to demoralize human beings than by promising them a better future and reneging on that promise. As with politicians who don't deliver on campaign promises, organizations that use the rhetoric of valuing diversity and avoid the substance eventually find that employee disillusionment and anger follow.

Employee disillusionment is not only a problem in companies that are not serious about culture change. This problem also occurs in organizations that begin with a legitimate, well-intentioned diversity initiative but then move on to "solve the problem" too quickly. Consider the following example:

BEEN THERE . . . DONE THAT

This mid-sized, high-technology company enjoys a reputation in its industry and on Wall Street as an organization "on the cutting edge of innovation." As such, it is a company that likes being the first to identify new opportunities and trends in research, product development, and management.

Because it has a multinational employee population and planned to build two additional plants in Asia before 1998, the company's HR department became interested in diversity about two years ago. After forming a multilevel, multicultural Diversity Task Force, the organization decided to commission an in-depth study of its culture and corporate environment. To assist with data collection, an external consulting firm was hired. Interview protocols were developed by the consultants and approved by the corporate Diversity Task Force. Finally, an invitation to participate was sent to every one of the 3,500 employees in the company. Of this total, 350 agreed to participate in focus groups or one-on-one interviews.

After four months of intensive data gathering, a 120-page document was produced, including 100 pages of verbatim comments from employees discussing their perceptions of the corporate culture. A list of follow-up recommendations was also delivered by the consultants to senior management and the Diversity Task Force. The list included more than 20 separate recommendations for changes in corporate strategic planning, marketing, communications, and performance review processes, as well as proposals for awareness training and the development of new recruitment, career pathing, and succession planning processes to broaden the candidate pool and help employees move laterally as well as upwardly in the organization.

A flurry of activity followed for the next nine months; then, the CEO announced that the diversity project was being brought to a successful close. In the eyes of senior management, the diversity problem was solved. It was now time to move on to the next competitive challenge.

The following week, the corporate Diversity Task Force announced that its work was now done. In a letter sent to every employee, the task force reiterated senior management's position on diversity, stating: "While we support diversity in our company, we do not want to see a bureaucracy develop just to maintain it. Nor do we want to give it disproportionate attention at a time when we face other competitive challenges. Henceforth, all matters pertaining to diversity management will be handled through normal HR channels."

Key Questions:

1. Based on your understanding of this implementation effort, is it likely that this Diversity Task Force's work is truly done?

2. How long do you anticipate it will take your own organization to fully adopt the value of diversity? Is leadership prepared to invest the time and resources required to do so?

When the concept of valuing diversity is first introduced in an organization, it is usually welcomed with interest and considerable senior management support. After all, the idea of maximizing the talents and skills of all employees is not one that business leaders usually oppose. As a first step, many organizations enthusiastically commit to studying the internal issues. However, because they do not recognize valuing diversity as a fundamental paradigm shift, companies are often not willing to invest the time and resources required for long-term, culture change. Yet, invariably, some substantive change *is* required to fully adopt the valuing diversity paradigm.

Investing Time and Dedicating Resources

Today, there are many successful entrepreneurial organizations that believe strongly in the merits of maintaining a lean corporate structure. Hence, when valuing diversity is introduced with its attendant needs for new methods and some management structure, it often stirs strong opposition. Because there is also a propensity for fast turnarounds and speed in problem solving in these companies, valuing diversity can also be viewed as overly cumbersome and complex. In fact, it may be both too cumbersome and complex to implement—when organizations are only interested in quick-fix solutions.

For organizations that regard three to six months as a long-term commitment, the length of time and the resources required for full adoption of the value of diversity are likely to be viewed as daunting, yet implementing this paradigm takes time. When it comes to valuing diversity, there is no quick fix and no free lunch. Without making a serious investment in both time and human resources, no company can fully adopt this paradigm. This does not mean that considerable progress cannot be made in the first year of diversity implementation, for it can be. But

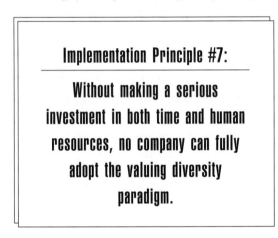

Implementation Principle #7:

Without making a serious investment in both time and human resources, no company can fully adopt the valuing diversity paradigm.

achieving the full benefits of diversity does not happen without dedicated resources and a strong corporate commitment to "stay the course" and pursue this goal well beyond the data-collection phase.

Like travelers who move quickly from place to place without taking time to pause and absorb the local customs and culture, some organizations are already saying "been there and done that" about valuing diversity. They are viewing this change as a short-term project of limited value and declaring their efforts finished long before they truly are. This premature closure virtually guarantees that these organizations will not retain any real benefit from their short-lived attempts at change. For valuing diversity can only flourish in an environment of sustained corporate support where executives are willing to commit to and invest in long-term change—rather than declare success prematurely.

NINE

Fueling Backlash

While interest in diversity implementation is increasing in organizations across every industry and sector, few institutions are prepared for the resistance that invariably follows the announcement of corporate support for this change. Like a pedestrian who steps off the curb without looking in either direction, companies are often blindsided by the backlash that is triggered when diversity implementation begins, yet, like death and taxes, backlash to change is inevitable. It is a predictable reaction to any new idea (particularly among skeptics and traditionalists) and occurs to some greater or lesser degree in all organizations.

Fear Fuels Backlash

Today, there are many reasons cited to explain the backlash—or resistance to valuing diversity—that inevitably erupts during implementation. Among those most commonly mentioned by the resisters themselves are: suspicion of otherness, politically correct intolerance, hiring quotas, reverse discrimination, a shrinking economic pie, divisiveness due to emphasis on differences over commonalties, the lowering of performance standards, brainwashing, mind control, violation of first amendments rights, the need for assimilation, and so on. While the list of opposing rationales runs the gamut from the seemingly reasonable to the ridiculous, all these explanations share a common trait. Each one is a fearful response to change.

Regardless of which particular reasons are offered, the common emotion that fuels the fire of backlash is fear. When individuals perceive diversity as a threat, they often react with denial, dread, hostility, cynicism, and/or contempt. Although they may not share the same reasons for being fearful, resisters can often create strong opposition when their fears increase, motivating them to bond with other resisters and unite against a common enemy. Generally, this united opposition is aimed at slowing down or stopping the adoption of change.

If it is recognized and carefully managed, backlash can be like a small bump in the road, momentarily disrupting the smooth, forward motion of the diversity implementation process; however, when it is not recognized, understood, or managed appropriately, it can become a major obstacle to change. In some cases, it can even become a countermovement that builds support and momentum for a very different goal—creating or maintaining an environment where diversity is suppressed or treated as a disruption and a problem.

Organizational Responses to Backlash

While some companies are beginning to acknowledge the need for increased understanding and proactive management of backlash, they remain the exceptions and not the rule today. Instead, most organizations are continuing to flounder in their attempts to manage this very real problem. Like pendulums swinging back and forth, they may deny the existence of the problem one day and then overreact to minor signs of resistance the next. As they grow more alarmed by continued opposition to change, many search for someone or something to blame. Finally, when they have failed in their attempts to placate or intimidate the dissatisfied, they may abandon the diversity effort entirely or greatly diminish its importance in order to appease the resisters.

As they move back and forth from no reaction to overreaction, few organizations recognize how inappropriate and poorly timed responses can often promote and increase backlash. They cannot see how they are throwing fuel on the flames of resistance even as they claim to be building support for the value of diversity. In addition, as they work at cross-purposes and sabotage their own efforts, they do not realize that every misstep reduces the probability that adoption of the value of diversity will occur. Consider the following organizational example:

APPEASING THE RESISTERS

Five years ago, this New England-based financial services firm was chosen as one of the "10 Best Employers for Diversity" by a prominent women's magazine. While the company had a strong, 20-year record of affirmative action and an excellent flexible benefits program, it had never gone public with these efforts. Instead, it had steadily worked over two decades to improve the corporate employee profile and create a more diversity-friendly environment.

However, after being selected by this magazine, it no longer seemed possible to work quietly for change. Now there was constant inquiry, particularly from client companies interested in finding out more about the corporate diversity initiative. The following year, another business publication featured the company in a cover story on "Diversity in the 1990s," and, thus, a star was born.

In an effort to live up to its growing image as a company on the leading edge of change, the organization stepped up its diversity awareness training. However, almost immediately after announcing that all managers would attend a two-day workshop, some backlash began to build.

Despite strong interest in attending, some of the management workshops appeared to be going badly. In one session, three white supervisors had objected to the training on the grounds that it violated their first amendment rights. In another workshop, there were accusations of political correctness from several participants and a strong negative reaction to a program segment dealing with cross-cultural communication and terms of respect. Following this incident, a letter of complaint signed by several employees and objecting to the training was sent to the CEO.

Alarmed by the backlash and fearing that the program was creating more problems than it was solving, the HR organization decided to quietly cancel the training. Despite the fact that this workshop had been successfully implemented in many other organizations, it was deemed too controversial to continue and was dropped.

In response to a torrent of queries from employees about the cancelation, the HR vice president issued a statement reiterating the company's support for diversity and reminding employees that "we have already done more to value diversity than any other company in our industry. Rather than continue offering a program that is viewed as divisive by some of our employees, we have decided to stop awareness training for now and pursue other management development activities instead."

Having canceled the program, HR was certain that the backlash would now stop; however, this turned out not to be the case. Instead, a month later, three employees sued the organization for harassment, claiming they were forced to attend awareness training and subjected to brainwashing. The lawsuit was reported in several business publications as an example of the abuses of diversity training. A year later, the suit was settled out of court. By that time, the entire diversity initiative had quietly disappeared from the corporate landscape.

Key Questions:

1. When backlash erupts, what can be the consequences to the change effort of fully meeting the demands of its resisters?
2. If this company had used the diversity adoption curve to target people for training, could it have minimized this backlash? How?

Despite the temptation that some managers and diversity specialists may have to turn and run at the first signs of resistance, it is counterproductive to deal with employee backlash by immediately recanting or caving in. While appeasement may quiet the skeptics and traditionalists for the moment, it will not defuse their fears. Instead, as in the case just described, it can often heighten apprehensions by reinforcing the fear that valuing diversity is dangerous and that the company's effort is out of control.

Unless an organization is prepared to give up entirely on valuing diversity, it can not afford to back away from the backlash that inevitably occurs in the early stages of implementation. If it does, it may decrease confidence in the change process among pragmatists as it reinforces resistance among skeptics and traditionalists.

Nor can an organization afford to directly challenge or confront such resistance whenever it occurs. While it may be tempting to insist that people just "get with the program" and accept the value of diversity, strong insistence can also undo implementation. If it is too emphatic or comes too early in the change process, it can undermine adoption by creating sympathy and support for the resisters.

Work with Those Who Are Ready

Instead of becoming discouraged, giving in, or reacting defensively to employee backlash, it is better to stay focused on the long-term goal of the change process: full adoption of the value of diversity. Beating backlash requires building support among those who are ready to adopt this paradigm while minimizing the early involvement of those who are still in resistance. This does not mean silencing the resisters. Instead, it means providing opportunities for dialogue about the value of diversity without coercing those who fear this change into participating or punishing them for their lack of involvement.

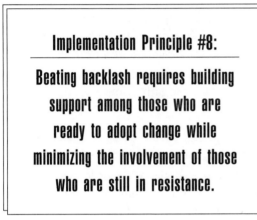

Implementation Principle #8:

Beating backlash requires building support among those who are ready to adopt change while minimizing the involvement of those who are still in resistance.

For many skeptics and traditionalists, backlash can be a reaction to forced, early participation in the change process. Once individuals become actively committed to resisting the value of diversity, it is far more difficult to convince them to embrace this change. Therefore, in the early stages of diversity implementation, it is unwise to insist on everyone's full participation, lest some choose to participate by actively opposing change.

Classic Mistakes That Fuel Backlash

While resistance often comes from employees who fear change, it can also be injected into the implementation process by managers and diversity specialists who are working their own agendas. In such cases, because of the blunders of those managing the change process, even supporters of the value of diversity will become resisters. *The Washington Post* recently discussed some of these self-induced problems in an article titled, "Diversity's Learning Curve: Multicultural Training's Challenges Include Undoing Its Own Mistakes." According to the article:

> Critics complain that the new and unregulated (diversity) industry too often has unqualified trainers, inadequate standards, excessive consultant fees and badly thought-out programs. Too often, critics contend, some early diversity programs were so aggressive and emotionally charged that they made workplace tensions worse, rather than better. The programs, many said, were better at inducing guilt than improving relations.[1]

The following section describes three of the classic change management errors that are having a negative impact on adoption in many organizations.

Marginalizing the Mainstream

One strategy guaranteed to close the door on full adoption of valuing diversity is leaving white men or white employees out of the change process. While it seems obvious that this large, powerful group must be included for change to be supported and fully adopted, in many organizations the mainstream is being ignored in efforts to value diversity. One small but telling measure of this exclusion is the way in which the term *diverse person* is used in organizations. When it is only used to refer to specific, underrepresented groups, such as women and people of color, and not to describe everyone, it leaves the mainstream out of the change process.

When valuing diversity is positioned as an effort aimed at benefiting women, people of color, people with disabilities, and others who may be perceived as outside the organizational mainstream, it becomes indistinguishable from affirmative action. At that point, most white men can no longer see any direct benefit associated with supporting this change. Does this mean that most oppose valuing diversity? No. However, when people believe they are ignored or excluded from full participation, they put less energy and less of themselves into making the process work. Ironically, while this very argument is often used to sell the concept of valuing diversity, it is seldom used to describe the need for including white men in the process.

To be fully adopted, valuing diversity must appeal to everyone's enlightened self-interest. It must benefit every employee and emphasize mutual respect and understanding for *all* core identity groups. While many organizations claim that their diversity initiatives are in the service of everyone, the absence of straight, white men from the planning, decision-making, and implementation processes often makes it clear that this is not really the case. What's more, if training used to reinforce the value of diversity targets white men as the problem, it will fuel backlash among members of this group. In addition, it is likely to create backlash among other employees who will view the demonization of white men as a sign of intolerance and write off the change process as hypocritical.

Backing Away from Sexual Orientation

Another threat to the change process that is building in many organizations today pertains specifically to the dimension of sexual orientation. While most companies understand that this is a core dimension of people's diversity, they are less inclined to defend the rights of gay, lesbian, and bisexual employees when they are threatened. Today, as organizations create antidiscrimination policies to protect the rights of gay and lesbian employees, they are coming under attack by community and religious groups opposed to this right. In addition, when the valuing diversity paradigm is introduced, there is often open opposition inside organizations to the rights of gay and lesbian employees to disclose their sexual orientation and to claim health benefits for their long-time partners.

These challenges cut to the very heart of what valuing diversity is about: the right of every individual to inclusion, respect, cooperation, and equal treatment. In cases where companies are reluctant to grant or protect the rights of gay and lesbian employees, they condone a double standard of unequal treatment for some. As such, they give tacit support to those groups and individuals who promote an agenda of hate—one that is in moral and ethical opposition to the value of diversity.

Today, homophobic backlash is creating fear in many organizations concerned that more conservative customers will abandon them if they speak out or stand up to pressure tactics and intimidation;

yet this is exactly what must occur if the change process is to succeed. When it comes to valuing diversity, organizations cannot reap the benefits that this new paradigm offers without providing the safe, supportive, and rewarding environment that all employees require to be full contributors.

Expertness and Moral Superiority

Finally, a discussion of the organizational causes of backlash would not be complete without some mention of the threats posed when expertness and moral superiority permeate the change process. In some organizations, where diversity efforts have spawned a cadre of project managers, facilitators, and implementers, there is a growing tendency among those in charge to exempt themselves from the need for increased awareness and understanding. Instead, some process managers are defining their role as expert and, occasionally, as righteous defenders of the way.

While there is always a need for expert knowledge, none of us can claim to be experts on diversity. The topic is simply too broad to be understood in the span of one lifetime. When facilitators of change position themselves as all-knowing or as morally superior, they shut off the dialogue that is a necessary step in the adoption process. Not only does this cause other people around them to shut down and back away from valuing diversity, it also closes the door on their own continued growth.

Today, in those organizations where righteousness and moral superiority abound, there is often a stifling silence that can be noted whenever the topic of valuing diversity is introduced. Since it is not safe to say what one really thinks or to voice objections concerning implementation, many people simply choose to say nothing. For those who know "the way" and wear the mantle of moral righteousness, this silence may be interpreted as agreement or support. But when this moral authority is not present and others feel free to comment, it becomes clear that stifling silence is often a measure of resentment and resistance.

To facilitate adoption of change, we must be open to hearing the views of everyone—including those of people who resist change. Open discussion and dialogue are a critical part of the adoption process. Without a safe environment and the free exchange of diverse opinions, mutual understanding and agreement become unattainable goals. What results instead is passive resistance and stifling silence.

Innovators and Change Agents Help Manage Resistance

Rather than take on the terrible burden of convincing those who fear change to embrace it, managers and facilitators of the change process must learn to use all their available resources to help defuse resistance and ready the organization. By using the Diversity Adoption Curve to plan and implement the change process, it is often easier to anticipate resistance and minimize its negative impact. If we recognize the varied stages of readiness that exist within each segment of the organization, we can create communications and develop educational programs that increase knowledge, comfort, and confidence as they reduce fear. Can we do this with a one-size-fits-all approach? Absolutely not!

Building Positive Momentum for Change

In the early stages of diversity implementation, all efforts should be aimed at building positive momentum for change. This means identifying those managers and employees most ready to embrace the value of diversity and providing them with the knowledge and skills required to make this new paradigm work. As these role models create success stories for others to see and emulate, interest among pragmatists will begin to grow. Instead of growing stronger, backlash will begin to fade as more employees witness and begin to experience the benefits of valuing diversity.

Thus, a wave-like approach to diversity implementation is required in order to build momentum and minimize backlash. Unlike top-down and bottom-up methods, this approach recognizes that *there are innovators, change agents, and pragmatists at every level of an organization* who can be instrumental in building support for change. It also acknowledges that skeptics and traditionalists exist at every level. Rather than presume that all those at the top (or at the bottom) of the organization are ready to embrace change, we can make more progress by understanding that some people in every group are ready and that some are not.

By working through the change agents and pragmatists to tell the valuing diversity story, we can disarm and defuse much of the backlash. By carefully managing the involvement of skeptics and traditionalists in the early stages of implementation, we can also minimize the enormous potential for fueling backlash within these segments. While every segment must be heard as the change process evolves, we can assure that discussion takes place in safe forums where everyone's issues are recognized and respected—regardless of which segment they are in.

Unfortunately, among many companies where diversity implementation has been underway for some time, experiences with backlash are often treated as closely guarded secrets. Instead of sharing experience to build a common knowledge base, many companies publicly deny the existence of this problem. It is as though any admission of resistance to this change would be an admission of failure. Yet, if the overall goal is to speed adoption of the value of diversity throughout the workplace, every organization and individual involved in managing this process would benefit from understanding more about backlash and from utilizing the Diversity Adoption Curve to manage and minimize it.

TEN

Minimizing the Business Case

In analyzing the efforts towards culture change taking place in organizations today, a strange paradox emerges: While a persuasive case can be made for the economic benefits of valuing diversity, this important outcome is seldom emphasized in most corporate initiatives. In fact, in many organizations it appears that the business case is deliberately left out of diversity discussions. Why would this powerful, persuasive argument be omitted so often in organizations that have growth and profitability at the top of their list of goals? A look back at the early days of the valuing diversity movement can provide valuable insights into the origins of this dichotomy. With the help of this historical perspective, it is easier to understand how the business case can be more effectively utilized in the pursuit of positive change.

Social Change Roots of Diversity Movement

Unlike total quality management, another fundamental change recently adopted in many companies, valuing diversity is seldom promoted in bottom-line terms. While increased competitive pressure, the need for innovation, and enhanced customer service are often referenced in diversity discussions, these arguments are seldom used as the primary drivers of this institutional change. Instead, proponents rush to claim the moral high ground and cite the compelling ethical rationale in support of diversity. What's more, in many organizations, there is a popular belief that emphasizing the business case will somehow diminish the power of the moral arguments for change. This aversion to leveraging the business case can be traced in large part to the origins of the valuing diversity movement.

Looking back at the last three decades in the American workplace, one sees that the valuing diversity movement began as an outgrowth of civil rights efforts to increase representation and fairness in our society. But while EO/AA efforts opened doors and provided increased access to the world of work for women and people of color during the 1970s, this access did not guarantee that development and respect would also be provided. Thus in the early 1980s, the need to *value* diversity emerged as a proactive response to a changing U.S. workforce and the limited ability of employment laws to assure inclusion, respect, and fair treatment.

As an extension of the social change movement of the 1960s and 1970s, valuing diversity is often viewed and positioned as a tool to help increase equity in the workplace. In most organizations, responsibility for implementing diversity has been assigned to EEO/AA managers—those with responsibility for enforcing nondiscrimination laws and fair employment policies. Given its history and intent, this positioning as an extension of EO/AA efforts makes good sense. However, this rationale often overshadows another equally compelling rationale. Instead of building a broad-based argument for the human *and* bottom-line benefits of valuing diversity, some diversity specialists perceive an inherent conflict between what is good for business and what is good for people. Others lack a strong business background and are often uncomfortable discussing diversity in terms of profit and loss. Among both groups, the economic case for valuing diversity is often underemphasized or completely ignored.

Business Value versus Human Value

Unlike many conflict situations where the interests of business and the interests of employees diverge and can be in strong opposition, there is no built-in dichotomy when it comes to valuing diversity. Instead, the benefits to organizations and individuals are closely aligned. There is a strong convergence of interests in adopting this change—the real promise of tangible gains for both individuals and institutions.

Because a welcoming and rewarding work environment produces superior human performance, it is in an employer's best interests to provide such an environment for employees. Because valuing diversity is a paradigm that can influence motivation and enhance innovation, it is a practical method for meeting the universal human need for inclusion and respect among customers and employees, thus improving productivity, customer satisfaction, and overall business growth. Yet, this pivotal and pragmatic argument is seldom voiced by the supporters of this change.

Emphasis on Moral Arguments

If you examine the case for valuing diversity that is used in organizations to persuade and convince people of the importance of full adoption, what you often find is a case that is heavily weighted with moral arguments. In most businesses, diversity is positioned in ethical terms as the right thing to do. An analysis of organizational problems often emphasizes the need for profile improvement and accelerated advancement for particular employee groups. In essence, an affirmative action argument is the one most often used to promote adoption.

While vague references may also be made to increased creativity and innovation, these benefits are usually framed as future outcomes. There is no attempt made to quantify the current benefits or to provide tangible examples and case histories that demonstrate how valuing diversity has actually enhanced creativity and improved output. Instead, managers and employees (including pragmatists, skeptics, and traditionalists) are expected to accept as an article of faith that this will occur someday.

Demographic Destiny

In addition to the moral argument for change, there is one quantitative argument related to changing workforce demographics that is often cited in support of valuing diversity. According to this argument, massive demographic shifts in the U.S. labor force before the year 2000 will necessitate that organizations value diversity, since the majority of new entrants into the labor force will be women, people of color, and immigrants. Unfortunately, while the projected shifts are enormous, numbers alone do not ensure that most organizations will embrace the value of diversity. On the contrary, it is just as likely that many institutions will view these changes as threatening and attempt to shoe-horn diverse people into established systems and modes of behavior. The fact that many organizations have been talking about these demographic changes for almost a decade but have done little or nothing to change their cultures is evidence of such a reaction.

Although workforce demographics are certainly a major factor in making the business case for valuing diversity, as a stand-alone argument, they have not motivated many organizations to change. Demographics alone do not build the case for creating a more open, flexible culture that can better integrate and leverage the skills of all people. This can only be accomplished by systematically compiling and publishing the positive business results that diversity delivers. It is precisely this type of concrete data that pragmatists often ask for as they consider adoption of the value of diversity.

Avoiding Bottom-Line Arguments

In our less-than-utopian world, where people rely more on practical, economic reasons to adopt change than moral or ethical ones, it would seem that most organizations are barking up the wrong tree by trying hard to convince pragmatists to embrace change based on its inherent morality. Instead of using morality as the sole motivator, what is also needed is a no-nonsense business case that points out how individuals, work teams, and organizations have benefited from valuing diversity in terms of enhanced teamwork, innovation, and profitability.

At this point, if you are beginning to resist this bottom-line appeal, I urge you to read on. Consider the following real-life situation where individuals committed to creating a corporate culture that valued diversity failed in their efforts because they focused only on the "soft" issues and provided no "hard" evidence of diversity's economic benefits:

PERCEPTION VERSUS REALITY

This industry leader is considered by most of its employees and competitors to have a "highly aggressive, kick-butt, hard-driving, arrogant, competitive, and somewhat macho culture." For most of the six white men in senior management, this characterization also describes their own management style—one that they believe has made the company what it is today—the industry leader. However, to many employees, this style creates serious "fit" issues and poses a threat to continued organizational effectiveness.

To help underscore the conflict between executive perceptions of the need for this style and employee perceptions, a study was commissioned to gather employee feedback about the corporate culture. A random sample of 25 percent of the organization participated in this qualitative research.

After results were compiled, the senior management team agreed to meet to review and discuss the findings. Off the record, several concluded in advance that the meeting would be a ridiculous waste of time; however, since the CEO wanted their participation, they had no choice but to attend.

During the one-day, off-site seminar, detailed feedback was presented regarding employee feelings about the company. Much criticism was directed at the overly competitive style that predominated. References were also made to "employees in pain," and to the "sense of alienation and exclusion" that many reported in the survey. To help persuade the group to adopt the value of diversity, the moral arguments for change were linked to these survey results.

As the day wore on, some of the executives continued to challenge the employee perceptions that were presented. The remainder fluctuated from appearing visibly annoyed to being bored by the discussion. Finally, about 30 minutes before the close of the day, the VP of marketing stated, "OK. OK . . . So we have some whiners in the organization who can't seem to cut it. What are we supposed to do—turn this company into a social club to make them feel better?

"Yes, we're a hard-driving organization. I, for one, am proud of that fact. That's what makes us profitable and successful. And if we could be realistic for a moment, I think we'd all agree that this is a business, not a social welfare agency. We're here to make a profit for ourselves and our shareholders.

"If someone could provide me with hard evidence of the economic benefits of diversity, I'd be very willing to listen. As it is, I think it's time we got back to work. And as for those people out there in so much 'pain,' perhaps it's time they considered looking elsewhere for employment. Regardless of their perceptions, we are very successful operating as we do. Why should we change?"

Key Questions:

1. In organizations just beginning the journey, where live examples of the value of diversity may still be rare, what other bottom-line evidence can be used to help build the positive business case?

2. How closely is the value of diversity linked to strategic business plans and bottom-line decisions in your organization?

3. Is valuing diversity viewed as a key component of marketing and customer service programs in your organization? If not, what can be done to build the business case for this paradigm?

While some innovators and change agents believe that the only real reason for valuing diversity is the moral reason, their efforts to accelerate adoption would be well served by a stronger economic case. Unfortunately, some individuals may view such arguments as crass, opportunistic, and heartless. As a result, they may find it difficult to speak with enthusiasm about the economic business case for valuing diversity. In addition, since much of the research being done to build support for change focuses on employee attitudes and feelings, it is difficult to make a strong dollars-and-cents argument. Nonetheless, those arguments are critical to full adoption. Without them, it is far less likely that the value of diversity will be fully recognized by the majority of people in the organization.

Minimize Turnover/Maximize Productivity

For those looking for hard numbers to support the value of diversity, an obvious place to start the search is within their own organizations. Each year, companies spend millions recruiting and training employees. To the extent that the work environment is not welcoming, there is a higher probability that *others* will leave. In such cases, turnover can become a costly and persistent problem, with the employer realizing a poor return on investment.

Even when turnover is relatively small, the unwillingness of a company to step up to valuing diversity issues can lower morale and productivity. In today's highly competitive business environment, organizations simply cannot afford to sacrifice any productivity; for even marginal declines can result in significant competitive disadvantage.

Customer Service Linkage

When it comes to the bottom-line arguments that can be used to help speed adoption of change, improved customer service may still be the most compelling and least leveraged argument of them all. Unfortunately, it seems many managers and diversity specialists still don't get this one. They do not make the connection between fostering a culture of understanding, respect, and cooperation and the ability of employees to interact effectively with diverse customers; nor do many help their organizations see this connection.

Today the maxim in successful organizations is "stay close to the customer." But how can organizations be confident that they are marketing, selling to, and interacting successfully with diverse customers if their employees deal with co-workers in a disrespectful or stereotypic manner?

If an organization has a high incidence of internal harassment complaints, can it feel confident that this is not a customer service issue, too? If employees are uncomfortable dealing with their openly gay co-workers, are they likely to be effective and respectful when dealing with customers or clients who are open about their different sexual orientation? In addition, are they likely to be maximizing important business opportunities with this group or any group that they have deep biases against? The obvious answer is no and this unfortunate fact can lead to serious problems. A recent case in point was the multimillion dollar racial-discrimination suit filed against Denny's by several African-American customers who were systematically locked out of the restaurant by company employees.[1]

Whether sanctioned by the organization or not, discriminatory practices are *always* costly. While they may not all lead to multi-million dollar lawsuits, they tarnish the image and reputation of an organization in the eyes of customers, investors, and potential employees. In a multicultural society like ours, biased behavior can and does impact the bottom line. It leads to lost sales, boycotts, and legal judgments that cost companies millions of dollars in lost revenues and settlements every year.

Ethnic Marketing

Today, companies intent on leveraging diversity in the marketplace must not only be concerned with limiting their liabilities, but they must also understand the particular consumer preferences of their diverse customers. According to *Time,* "By the year 2000, minorities may account for 30 percent of the U.S. economy. Major corporations like Pepsico, K Mart, and J.C. Penney are going all out to win over free-spending ethnic consumers, recruiting minority marketing experts who speak each group's language and know their customs . . . Mass marketing worked when America was a cultural melting pot. But now you need a different message to suit the taste of each group."[2]

This growing awareness of the spending power of ethnic groups is causing many organizations to take the business case for valuing diversity more seriously. In the future, it is likely that interest in targeted marketing based on ethnicity and other dimensions of diversity will continue to grow in most organizations. As data-based marketing techniques become more sophisticated, diverse market segments are easier to identify. Once identified, it is then possible to appeal to many segments in separate and distinct ways, provided there is a depth of knowledge about each targeted group within the organization. Thus, the more knowledge institutions acquire about their diverse customers and clients, the more successful they can potentially be in customizing and personalizing their marketing messages.

A False Dichotomy

To create momentum for change, it is time to challenge the false assumption that what is good for business is bad for people. In the case of valuing diversity, there is a different truth. Unlike many examples of changes that benefit either the organization or employees, valuing diversity can truly benefit both. In many respects, this paradigm provides organizations with a wonderful and somewhat rare opportunity to do what's best for employees and reap greater profits as a result. This strong alignment between the business benefits and the human benefits makes the case for valuing diversity more compelling.

Business Benefits Strengthen the Case

Unlike win-lose situations in which we succeed by causing others to fail, the valuing diversity paradigm can create many winners in an organization. Ultimately, it can help both individuals and organizations exceed their highest expectations and succeed as never before.

> ### Implementation Principle #9:
>
> **It is critical that we now develop the strategic and financial arguments for valuing diversity, for building the business case strengthens the probability of full adoption.**

Because it is a new paradigm, valuing diversity has yet to be fully adopted in any organization; therefore, many of its benefits have yet to be realized. It is time to look at the broad potential that this change offers *organizations and individuals.*

It is critical that we now develop the strategic and financial arguments for valuing diversity. For building the business case strengthens the probability of full adoption and thus improves the likelihood that every employee and customer alike will benefit from this important change.

ELEVEN

Awareness Training: Panacea and Problem

As organizations implement diversity, a variety of activities are required to ready the environment, build support, and sow the seeds of change. One important component of this implementation process is awareness training. Unlike skills training that develops and hones specific behaviors required for mastery of a task, awareness training is broader in scope. While it may include some skill-based learning, much of it tends to focus on prejudice identification, bias reduction, and empathy building. It is training aimed at helping people see and understand the world of work from the perspectives of *others*—people of different core identities.

Goals of Awareness Training

In order to increase empathy and cross-cultural understanding, awareness training encourages people to share personal histories and compare their own experiences with those of *others*. An underlying assumption of this training is that individuals who participate can increase their knowledge, ability to empathize, and their understanding of the differential impact of the corporate culture by sharing stories and hearing about *others'* experiences, frustrations, challenges, and joys.

Many people who attend awareness training for the first time report an intense and powerful learning experience. Awareness training deals with the emotional as well as the rational content of human interactions; it probes and explores the way people feel as well as the way people act. Because it engages both the head and the heart, awareness training often elicits strong personal reactions and, as a result, can be an especially exciting and involving way to learn about cultural diversity. In the immediate aftermath, it is not unusual to hear participants describe this training as one of the most insightful and pivotal events in their lives.

Preparing Employees for Change

Since most people enter the workplace with a multicultural knowledge deficiency, they are often unaware and uncomfortable when dealing with *others* of diverse core identities. Even though they may all speak the same language and live in the same town, differences in race, religion, ethnicity, gender, sexual orientation, physical abilities, education, and income can create vast gaps in experience and understanding among co-workers in the same work group. To build support for valuing diversity and help bridge these gaps, awareness training is often used to introduce employees to the benefits of understanding and respecting cultural diversity. But while this training can increase openness and support for change, it is not a panacea. The following case history illustrates what often happens when awareness training is used as a blanket solution to diversity management problems:

GREAT EXPECTATIONS . . . DISAPPOINTING RESULTS

This division of a large international food company was invited to preview a new diversity training program that had recently been purchased by the corporate education department. Having read a bit about diversity training, Melissa, the new HR vice president, decided to attend the pilot program.

Upon arrival, Melissa was surprised to see every major division in the company represented at the session. Judging by the strong attendance, it seemed that diversity was catching on in other departments. Unlike the rumors she had occasionally heard about white male bashing at diversity training, this program actually seemed to build a rapport among all the participants. As the day progressed, people became more open, more comfortable with the basic message: the importance of mutual respect and cooperation in building productive work teams.

At the conclusion of the session, Melissa heard several participants comment on what a productive and eye-opening session it had been. Based on her own experience, as well as other participants' feedback, she left the workshop convinced that her division should immediately move ahead with the training—or risk being left in the dust by the other operating units.

Since her organization had a reputation in the company for being slow to change with changing times, she also thought the introduction of diversity training might help to alter this image. In addition, the training could enhance employee teamwork by promoting mutual respect and encouraging employees to "do the right thing." Based on the large number of complaints her group was receiving from employees about harassment, anything that could be done to ease the tension would be worthwhile.

Since Melissa's boss was also very new to the division, he was eager to follow her recommendation; thus, the awareness workshops were started in the spring of 1992. To help deliver the programs, 12 employee volunteers were sent to facilitator training classes and certified to co-lead the workshop with an external consultant as their partner. Participant feedback about the program and the facilitators was also collected at the close of each workshop, and these evaluations were closely monitored by Melissa's office. Generally, reactions from participants were very favorable regarding course content and trainer effectiveness. It seemed to Melissa that the training was going very well.

Two years later, after all 1,400 employees from the division had attended the program, a follow-up study was commissioned by the organization to measure the impact of the training. While most employees reported enjoying the class and some stated their personal behavior had changed, few perceived that the work environment was any different as a result. Based on this feedback, Melissa sent a letter to the corporate training department expressing her "disappointment. Since the program did not lead to significant change, it was obviously not an effective class."

Key Questions:

1. What other steps could have been taken in this division to ready the environment—prior to introducing awareness training?

2. Is mass training for all employees an effective way to alter the corporate environment? What other actions might be taken instead? In addition to training?

Regardless of how involving or experiential the design may be, awareness training cannot perform miracles. For most human beings, even very powerful emotional experiences fade with the passage of time. As people return to their familiar, everyday world, they tend to fall back on familiar assumptions, behavior patterns, and attitudes. Unless their new learnings are regularly and formally reinforced, this one-time-only event will seldom lead to lasting behavior change. What's more, even when individuals are changed by their experiences in training, there is no reason to assume that the organization will be!

Although individuals often report a change in personal consciousness as a result of attending awareness training, their insights are seldom powerful enough to influence or alter embedded assumptions, practices, and norms that exist in the corporate environment. While heightened awareness can create the internal motivation required for change, it is ongoing communication, education, behavior reinforcement, recognition and reward, leadership commitment, and supportive policies and practices that together create deep and lasting culture change.

> **Implementation Principle #10:**
>
> **While excellent training alone will not assure culture change, inappropriate training can do considerable damage to diversity implementation efforts.**

Individuals who have a powerful awakening in training and leave with important new insights and heightened sensitivity can often be called on to support systems change, but they cannot be expected to make change happen on their own. While some may try, they quickly discover that old habits and assumptions live on. What's more, the insights gained in awareness training can actually create new conflicts for people—if they return to a business-as-usual work environment where diversity is still not recognized or valued.

While excellent training alone will not assure culture change, inappropriate training can do considerable damage to implementation efforts. Consider the following case history:

STIRRING THE POT

More than 20 years ago, this company began offering a workshop to help employees examine the origins and impact of racial prejudice and racism. In many respects, it was a ground-breaking effort, since few companies were doing anything to proactively address this issue at the time. Borrowing from the encounter-group training models popular in the 1960s and 1970s, the program encouraged open, candid discussion and disagreement among participants.

At first, the workshop trainers remained neutral during the more heated employee interactions. However, in later workshops, they routinely played the role of challenger. In order to help stir the pot and precipitate break-through insights, some trainers would aggressively take on individual participants in front of the entire group. Often, this resulted in heightened tension, confrontation, and divisiveness within the group.

While some employees described their experiences at these workshops as one of the most significant events of a lifetime, others termed the training excessive, accusatory, and punishing. As feedback about the confrontational nature of the experience circulated throughout the company, many employees avoided attending. Others who were forced to attend often became openly opposed to the program afterwards and lobbied hard for discontinuing the training. Finally, after receiving many complaints, the workshop was canceled and other less confrontational programs followed.

Then in 1992 a highly publicized racial discrimination suit was filed against the company. As a result, internal efforts were stepped up to raise management awareness. After considering several options, the training department decided to reintroduce the same racial awareness program. When asked why they had decided to use the old design once again, one trainer stated, "Because management still doesn't 'get it' on racism and this is the best method we have for waking them up."

Amidst objections from many, the program was put back in operation, using the same design that had been used in the 1970s version. In most departments, managers were told that attendance was mandatory.

Key Questions:

1. Based on the early experiences of companies that piloted diversity training, what has been learned about the appropriate role of the trainer?

2. Why are some diversity awareness programs viewed as life-changing events by some participants and as bashing by others?

3. Are confrontation and intimidation useful methods for building support for the value of diversity?

Diversity Training's Confrontational Past

Back in the 1970s when awareness training was very new and virtually untried in most organizations, some attempts to wake people up were akin to throwing cold water on a sleeping giant. The uproar that often followed was not worth the time, energy, or effort expended. Nonetheless, many companies with good intentions believed in the value of high-impact training and experimented with different and sometimes counterproductive methods. Frequently, in attempts to surface the real issues, some trainers elected to play the challenger role—often overplaying it. Instead of increasing understanding and awareness, this method of facilitation often led to polarization among participants and increased backlash. As they became more active, controlling, and involved in the content of the workshop discussions, these trainers often increased unease and stress within the group and on occasion caused some participants to take their early leave.

Blame and Guilt as Motivators

While some early training programs were often laced with heavy doses of finger-pointing, most organizations quickly discovered that blame and guilt were not highly effective methods for motivating people to change their values or behavior. Although research has shown that both blame and guilt *can* cause some individuals to modify biased behavior, these same methods have been proven to backfire with others. This problem was confirmed in a recent *Training & Development* article on diversity training. According to the article: "Training that appeared to beat up on men bred resentment, fear, and eventually backlash—and not just from white men . . . This approach reinforced the 'us versus them' view, which made everybody feel victimized and disempowered."[1] What's more, it is often those with the most deeply ingrained prejudices who seem to benefit the least or not at all from exposure to these tactics.[2] Attempting to make such individuals feel personal responsibility or guilt usually elicits the opposite reaction: It causes them to become more hostile and adamant in their opposition to change.

Designing Effective Training

While some mistakes made in the 1970s and 1980s were due to inexperience, today far more is known about what makes awareness training effective. To avoid backlash, training must be built around a broad definition of diversity that includes everyone. To attract the pragmatists, it must be tied to business results. To be consistent with the philosophy of valuing diversity, both the awareness training design and the trainers must model and encourage respect, cooperation, openness, and increased understanding. Finally, while building understanding and empathy is appropriate at the start of implementation, a full educational curriculum for managing and leveraging diversity must also be developed over time to include skills training aimed at behavior change.

Selecting and Preparing Trainers

Sometimes a solid training program with the right kind of institutional support can still backfire—if the trainers are poorly prepared for their role. While some companies use only external training consultants to assure a high standard of professionalism at every workshop, these trainers often know little about the particular organization, its culture, or its employees. Hence, the examples and references used in workshops may be overly generic. What's more, external trainers may have little expertise as change management consultants and little understanding of what is required to create a culture that values diversity. Out of the classroom environment, many lack the knowledge and experience needed to serve as expert resources on matters of culture change.

As an alternative to using external trainers, more organizations are now encouraging employees to step forward as volunteer facilitators. When adequate training is provided to prepare people for their role, this approach can be quite effective. Involvement of change agents in the education process can be a powerful way to build momentum and support among other segments of the organization.

Unfortunately, in some companies, adequate training is not provided for these volunteers. As a result, many inexperienced facilitators are finding themselves in over their heads—floundering to answer participant questions and attempting to lead discussions with a knowledge and experience base that is a mile wide and an inch deep.

Today, more organizations are moving to a model of internal and external trainer pairs, where the group facilitation skills of the external trainer balance out the corporate knowledge and experience of the internal trainer. While all three of these staffing approaches can and do work, this method seems to be the one with the lowest potential for failure due to gaps in corporate knowledge, understanding of diversity issues, or training expertise.

Selecting Participants

As discussed earlier in this chapter, not every employee is a good candidate for awareness training. In fact, one can predict with a high level of certainty that such experiential learning will be inappropriate or even counterproductive for a large percentage of employees in every organization. Ironically, the surest way to assure failure for awareness training is to insist on universal participation during the early stages of implementation. In such situations, angry traditionalists and skeptics, coerced into participating against their will, are very likely to have negative reactions. What's more, their open resistance to the training can be a divisive and disruptive influence in group settings, diminishing the impact of the learning experience for other interested participants.

Initially, awareness training should be targeted at innovators and change agents. At a later stage of implementation (in years two through four), this pool can be expanded to include all pragmatists. Since change agents and innovators are positively predisposed towards valuing diversity, a self-identification process is usually very effective in identifying who is ready now for training. As news of the training spreads throughout the organization, change agents, in particular, are likely to come forward and volunteer as participants and facilitators. Grouped with other individuals of similar predisposition, their training experience is more likely to be positive and empowering. As a result, they will return to their respective work groups as powerful and persuasive catalysts for change.

Part of the Problem or Part of the Solution?

Despite the missteps that have occurred along the way, awareness training is playing a pivotal role in virtually every successful implementation effort in organizations. But it is by no means a stand-alone solution or panacea. On the contrary, when not properly administered, awareness training can have a pervasive, negative impact. To paraphrase a famous line: "It can become part of the problem, instead of being an important part of the solution."

TWELVE

Some Things Not Worth Doing Are Not Worth Doing Well

As companies implement diversity, a variety of activities are required to ready the environment, build support and knowledge among employees, and redirect organizational efforts towards the goal of valuing and leveraging differences. Among the many initiatives that have been started to achieve these purposes, several are gaining popularity in organizations despite their consistently disastrous impact where tried.

While often accompanied by good intentions, these initiatives suggest a restatement of the old adage "Something worth doing is worth doing well." In each of these cases, "Something not worth doing is not worth doing well." Even when they are thoroughly planned and efficiently executed, these activities invariably lead to a slowing of change adoption and a strengthening of backlash. This happens because these activities lose sight of the goals of valuing diversity. Instead of being the means to an end, they become ends in themselves with their own independent agendas. Rather than fostering cooperation, unification, and clarity of purpose, they promote fragmentation, Balkanization, and confusion. This chapter will discuss several of the most prevalent of these well-meaning but misdirected activities.

Adversarial Affinity Groups

As awareness and understanding begin to build inside organizations, a strong call for informal networking and support is often heard from women, people of color, and other groups historically viewed as outside the cultural mainstream. This desire for increased contact with and support from one's own core identity group is a very real need that many individuals have. Not surprisingly, it often emerges among women, people of color, gay men and lesbians, and so on, when an organization begins to move away from assimilation as the model for managing core differences towards valuing diversity. At this point, some employees begin to openly reach out towards others of similar core identities. No longer concerned about being seen together or about learning to fit in, each now has a curiosity and a desire to connect and share experiences with "other people like me."

Filling A Critical Need

Affinity groups based on core differences such as race, ethnicity, age, sexual orientation, and gender can fill many important needs for some employees. They can be important sources of comfort, inclusion, information, advice, social connection, and sanity checks—providing much of what is typically required to succeed in the business world. Among many *others* outside the mainstream who may be isolated and less able to obtain support and validation from their mainstream colleagues, connecting with people of similar core identity is critical for survival, renewal, and long-term success.

While institutions routinely resisted employees' demands for affinity groups before valuing diversity, those embarked on culture change now often encourage the formation of these self-help networks. As organizations recognize the need that every group has for self-validation, support, and role models, many realize that affinity groups can play an important part in providing these.

From Allies to Adversaries

Yet, at some corporations, where affinity groups were once welcomed and encouraged by the organization, there is now an undertone of resentment and hostility surrounding them. No longer viewed as informational resources and informal networks, in some companies, affinity networks have become institutionalized special interest groups with independent agendas that are not tied to valuing diversity. In fact, their charters often work at cross-purposes with the change process, occasionally sabotaging the broader effort. What causes this transformation from ally to adversary? It often results from an organization's benign neglect (i.e., the lack of meaningful interaction with these groups). When senior management displays polite disregard for the work of affinity groups, an "us versus them" relationship can and often does develop. In other cases, it can be the group's single-issue perspective that causes it to become too internally focused, isolated from the broader organizational goal of culture change and competitive with other employee networks.

While some organizations have done an excellent job of involving affinity groups in the planning of long-term culture change, other companies less knowledgeable about how to proceed or less committed to valuing diversity disengage from these groups once they are formed. As meaningful dialogue with senior management grows more limited or becomes nonexistent, these networks become isolated and cynical about the organization's commitment. Nonetheless, many do not disband. Instead, as their memberships grow, the groups begin to redefine their role and mission. No longer focused on informal networking, culture change, and valuing diversity, they now focus on "getting whatever we can for our own constituency." As such, they become special interest groups that often have enough power to make trouble for the organization and thereby intimidate it into granting limited concessions.

Special Interest Advocacy

Once they redefine their roles as special interest advocates, their interest in partnering with other affinity groups and the organization itself is limited by the fear that cooperation will dilute their power. Ironically, this reluctance to partner and share power often mirrors the original problem that valuing diversity was attempting to correct.

When they veer off their intended course, affinity groups can increase the problems of elitism, fragmentation, and infighting that often exist in organizations where diversity is not valued. As such they become yet another organizational problem. Regardless of how large they grow or how organized and powerful they become, adversarial affinity groups do not advance the goals of mutual respect, cooperation, and trust that form the foundation of all valuing diversity efforts; therefore, they are truly something not worth doing.

In order to avoid this problem, organizations must play an active role in both the chartering and ongoing work of all affinity groups. To the extent that they exist to meet the career development needs of employees, company-sanctioned affinity groups serve two constituencies: the members and the organization. When their goals are in alignment with the organization's, they can be powerful partners in the change process, providing input from their constituencies and working with other groups to build common ground. However, when their goals are in opposition to the organization's goal of valuing diversity, they cease to be a force for cooperation and productive change, regardless of how righteous their motives are.

Diversity Apologists

As the media discourse about diversity becomes more intense and at times more distorted, some organizations are growing concerned about their public association with this "politically hot" topic. When their own understanding of and commitment to valuing diversity are weak, organizations will sometimes distort and exaggerate the potential risks of embracing this change. Consider the following case history:

DAMNING WITH FAINT PRAISE

This successful accounting firm determined that a diversity initiative was needed to attract a broader client base and compete for talent in the employment marketplace. In order to send the right signal to the organization about the importance of this new firm priority, a highly visible Executive Diversity Council (EDC) was created to craft a valuing diversity vision and set strategy. The council consisted of seven senior partners—powerful men and women who were well respected throughout the firm.

As its first official act, the EDC agreed to meet for a full day to develop a corporate diversity vision. But as this planning session wore on with members continually challenging and disagreeing, it became clear that the group was not ready to develop or commit to anything. Strong differences of opinion existed among members about what diversity was and what the scope of the initiative should be.

Other meetings followed, with several ending in total frustration as people polarized around issues such as "political correctness," "quotas," and "white male bashing." Among several members of the group, these issues were viewed as potential outcomes of a misdirected effort—outcomes that the entire group agreed it would do everything possible to avoid.

Once the five pragmatists and skeptics on the EDC were assured by others that valuing diversity would not lead to excesses and abuses in the organization, the work of crafting a corporate vision statement began again. This time, to help speed the process, one skeptic member offered to create a draft that included the group's best thinking on diversity to date. With the help of minutes from previous meetings, this member developed a one-page aspiration statement entitled "What Diversity Can Be and What It Will Not Be." While diversity was described as a potential competitive advantage in the statement, much of the document emphasized what diversity would not become in the firm. In particular, the statement proclaimed that "valuing diversity will not become an exercise in political correctness, white male bashing, reverse discrimination, or hiring quotas."

After reviewing this draft at their next EDC meeting, the group became embroiled in yet another conflict. This time, members polarized around the apologist tone of the statement. While some deemed the tone reassuring, one called it "overly negative" and another stated, "It's a political nightmare rather than a corporate vision."

Despite these objections, the council voted to approve the document and published it widely throughout the organization. As a result of this publication, awareness of diversity increased significantly throughout the firm. But while the statement focused attention on the new corporate initiative, it also increased polarization, convincing many skeptics and traditionalists that diversity posed potential threats to the firm and added little value.

Key Questions:

1. What would an appropriate statement of corporate support for diversity say about issues such as political correctness, and reverse discrimination?

2. Should position on the Diversity Adoption Curve be a factor in selecting individuals for membership on an executive diversity council?

While leadership involvement in implementation planning is essential for long-term success, it is the early involvement of innovators, change agents, and then pragmatists that will set the most appropriate tone for change. When executive diversity committees are convened based upon level *only*, with little thought given to levels of understanding and commitment, they can be overly populated with skeptics and traditionalists. When this occurs, they can become apologists for the diversity effort, minimizing its positive potential and magnifying bogus issues such as reverse discrimination and white male bashing. As such, these committees are something not worth doing. Instead of building commitment to the new paradigm, they build anxiety in the organization that, with more strategic leadership, can be minimized.

Training as Punishment or "PYA" Program

While problems inherent in mandatory awareness training are discussed in Chapter 9, two recent scandals involving diversity training in the public and private sectors prompt the inclusion of this section on training not worth doing. In one widely publicized case, a workshop at a federal agency was designed so that male participants would experience what sexual harassment was like—by being forced to walk through a gauntlet of women who were encouraged to fondle and leer at the men as they passed. This excessive example of an exercise not worth doing led to an unfair labor practice complaint and a great deal of negative publicity for the agency involved.

In another incident at a large food company, diversity awareness training was presented as a legalistic, protect-the-company solution to several serious employee discrimination complaints. Rather than involve employee volunteers to facilitate open discussion, awareness workshops were presented by the company's legal department. This, in turn, created doubt and suspicion among participants about the corporate intent behind the training. Was the training designed to increase awareness and understanding or was it merely a "pya" strategy? Regardless of the answer, it failed in its attempt at conciliation and, instead, exacerbated tensions within the company. Eventually, employees used information collected from these workshops to prove bias and employment discrimination in a now infamous court case.

Whether the goal is punishment or pya, awareness training done for either of these reasons is never worth doing. While employees may be more understanding of lapses between the goals and the outcome of quality training, they are less likely to sit still for valuing diversity training that devalues or manipulates them. An organization that uses awareness training to protect itself from lawsuits or that permits employees to be insulted in workshops in order to make a learning point, runs a serious legal and ethical risk. Rather than make matters worse, they would be better served to forgo such training entirely.

Diversity Committees without Charter or Clout

As the pressure to "do something" about diversity mounts, many organizations respond in the quintessential bureaucratic manner: they form committees to study the situation. Whereas before there was no organized effort to understand the issues or plan a strategy, now diversity committees pop up in every department, division, and business unit. Often, these committees result from the downward delegation of ambiguity. Since most senior managers are not sure what to do about diversity, they pass the project on by "empowering" a task force of employees to go figure it out.

Once these task forces and councils form, they often spend anywhere from a year to three years attempting to define their role and mission. Not surprisingly, many eventually disband because of frustration and lack of clarity surrounding their charter. Others become activity-focused—planning ethnic food events, film festivals, and other multicultural celebrations without ever focusing on the goals of organization culture change. While these committees may add some gastronomic value by enhancing awareness of ethnic cuisines among employees, they are often not worth having if they distract the organization from the real work of culture change. Consider this example of good intentions and a disappointing outcome:

In Search of a Purpose

Sixteen months ago, after being acquired by a company that was "big on diversity," this engineering organization of 4,000 people was pressured into forming a Diversity Core Team (DCT). The DCT consisted of eight racially diverse men and women, only one of whom had any management experience. After four frustrating meetings to get organized, a chairperson was finally chosen to help guide the team process. Then the group turned its attention to its charter.

During the next several meetings, members talked about what they thought senior management wanted them to do. As the discussions continued, it was clear that each person held a different opinion about the "what." In order to clarify expectations, the chair agreed to solicit input from top management and report back. But scheduling meetings with this busy group was extremely difficult, and after three more months, the team still lacked concrete input and direction.

By this time, every DCT member was being asked, "Exactly what are you doing on that team?" It seemed both their colleagues and supervisors had begun to notice that no visible actions were resulting from their monthly, four-hour meetings. Although DCT members believed they were working hard, most were uncomfortable answering their colleagues' questions. There was simply nothing specific to report.

Then, 10 months into the process, one member suggested that the DCT host an annual diversity conference. Relieved to finally have a concrete, actionable suggestion, the group immediately seized upon this idea and set about the business of planning the event. As they proceeded, members found many obstacles in their path: no department budget for funding the conference; no ongoing administrative support to assist with planning; little interest from the leadership in participating; schedule conflicts; lack of support from their own managers, who regularly objected to the amount of time required for planning; no tie-in to other diversity activities happening elsewhere in the company, and so on.

As each new hurdle appeared, there were arguments among the members about how to proceed. Often during their meetings, someone would storm out of the conference room or break down in tears. As the date of the conference drew near, several members resolved that they were stepping down from the DCT as soon as the conference was over. As one woman stated, "This has been the most confused, frustrating experience of my life. Why would I want to continue being involved?"

Despite mounting frustration, the meeting finally came to pass and 125 employees attended. At the closing session, DCT members received a letter of commendation from the department's executive committee thanking them for their "efforts to make diversity part of our culture" and encouraging them to continue their work.

Encouraged by this gesture of support, everyone decided to return to the DCT for another year. No longer frustrated by a lack of focus, the team now understood what it was supposed to do: plan an annual three-day diversity conference for 125 to 200 people.

Key Questions:

1. Assuming that the DCT remains focused on annual conference planning, what will be its long-term prospects for promoting deep culture change?

2. What could have been done by the members and the organization to make this group more effective?

3. What were some of the planning steps that the group overlooked during its eight-month start-up phase?

To succeed at transforming the organization culture, diversity committees must approach their work as they would any other business task: with clear objectives, strategies, and the required mix of management skills and experience. They must begin with a broad charter endorsed by the leadership of the organization. Their membership must include people in visible leadership roles, people with change management expertise as well as employees who are personally interested in and knowledgeable about cultural diversity. Early in the life of the group, a multiyear strategic plan must be developed outlining goals and roles. Survey data must be gathered to validate and help operationalize the plan. The business case for valuing diversity must be clearly understood and communicated throughout the organization. Committee members must also commit to ongoing education in order to become more knowledgeable about diversity issues and organizational opportunities. And all this should be done before any massive program, event, or conference is even discussed!

Sadly, the experiences of the team described in this case history are common in many organizations today. When the need to act overwhelms the long-term purpose of a valuing diversity initiative, what often results is a splashy annual event rather than a detailed, multiyear plan. While some would argue that an annual conference focused on valuing diversity is worth doing because it is still better than doing nothing, this is very debatable. For when the annual event displaces a comprehensive, systemic approach to culture change, it becomes an organizational distraction that actually slows adoption.

Lack of Integration across Working Committees

In larger organizations, where there are often many local diversity committees, the lack of purpose and direction that these committees grapple with can also lead to another difficulty later in the implementation process. When multiple committees work in isolation, they often develop different visions, many definitions of diversity, and different overall objectives. Once each team agrees on where it is going, many are then reluctant to modify their approach in order to better integrate efforts across the entire organization. Rather than coordinate their activities, they can wind up working at cross-purposes with each other by offering competitive events and insisting that "ours is better than yours."

When coordination and careful planning are given priority over fast action, many of these committee management problems can be avoided. But resisting the temptation to "give them what they want" rather than what the organization needs is never easy. It requires vision, organizational clout, and a strong sense of resolve. Since many diversity committees lack one or several of these, they continue to put fast action and visible activity before the need for comprehensive, long-term change. As such they provide a distraction from the need for culture change rather than a long-term solution.

Color Coding and Oppression Hierarchies

Since valuing diversity was first introduced into organizations in the 1980s, it has been continually confused with affirmative action. While we have already discussed the importance of separating these distinctly different efforts, there is one action occurring today in many companies that contributes to employee confusion about what valuing diversity is and whom it benefits. That is the tendency of many people of *every* racial group to turn the topic of valuing diversity into a color-coded discussion.

Because racism remains one of the most toxic, lethal, and emotionally charged problems in our society, it can frequently overwhelm valuing diversity initiatives in the workplace. When this occurs, an oppression hierarchy results: race becomes the single core dimension that the organization focuses on, and all other dimensions recede into the background. While the persistence of racism in most organizations makes this reaction understandable, it is nonetheless a response that delimits the potential that valuing diversity has to address multidimensional issues simultaneously, to build common ground across all groups, and thereby achieve full adoption more rapidly.

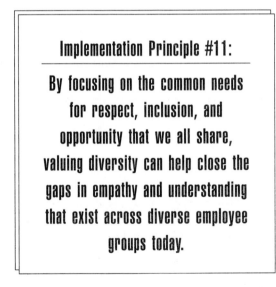

Implementation Principle #11:

By focusing on the common needs for respect, inclusion, and opportunity that we all share, valuing diversity can help close the gaps in empathy and understanding that exist across diverse employee groups today.

Although it is sometimes tempting to create an oppression hierarchy in order to allocate limited resources, this is another action not worth taking. Instead of building broad support for change, such hierarchies often lead to reduced interest and involvement among those whose core issues are ranked lowest on the list. Rather than prioritize and address destructive "isms" one at a time, valuing diversity has the power to do much more. When it is inclusive of all groups, this change offers real benefit to every individual. Only when all employees see themselves as potential beneficiaries can valuing diversity receive the broad-based support required for full adoption. And as the culture of respect, inclusion, and cooperation begins to solidify, gaps in empathy and understanding between diverse groups can finally begin to close.

Wholistic Advocacy

To avoid oppression hierarchies and increase cross-cultural empathy and understanding, facilitators of this change must also become *wholistic* supporters of the value of diversity. As such, they must be passionate advocates of inclusion, respect, and cooperation for *others,* as well as for themselves and the groups to which they belong. While this may be relatively easy to understand, it is never easy to do; for what attracts many to the work of culture change is often "what's in it for me and people like me."

To achieve the goal of full adoption, facilitators must understand the basic issues and then serve the needs of *all* core identity groups—not only those to which they belong. Working only in the service of one's own group is both selfish and self-serving. As such it is something not worth doing. In contrast, advocating as strongly for fairness and respect for *others* as for ourselves is the purest and most powerful expression of valuing diversity. It is something definitely worth doing well.

Flawless Implementation

As with any new innovative effort, diversity implementation can never be totally predictable. There are simply too many variables to manage in too short a time and usually with limited resources. Regardless of the degree of planning that may take place, there are always occasional bumps in the road as the change process unfolds. This is an inevitable fact of diversity implementation.

However, despite this inevitability, some organizations still start the journey expecting flawless implementation. Because it can stifle innovation and engender fear, this expectation is also something not worth having. Rather than stymie creativity and experimentation, organizations can best support diversity implementation by providing education and ongoing support for the implementers and a foundation of mutual respect, inclusion, and cooperation for their work.

THREE

Accelerating Change

THIRTEEN

Laying the Groundwork for Change

In Section 1 of this book, we focused on the fundamentals of valuing diversity and the basic dynamics involved in introducing this change in organizations. In Section 2, we reviewed several of the classic mistakes occurring in organizations where valuing diversity efforts are already under way. At this point, it should be apparent that despite the best of intentions, successful diversity implementation can be a complex and challenging task.

Having focused on many of the problems and the pitfalls, it is now time to move on to an exploration of successful implementation strategies. For despite the obvious difficulties, the vision of valuing diversity can become a reality. In fact, experiences in some organizations today indicate that diversity implementation efforts are already becoming successful. By examining the collective experience and learning occurring in these organizations, we can identify several important steps that can and must be taken. In this final section, we will outline those important steps and discuss how implementation can be done to minimize problems and maximize prospects for full adoption of change.

Before Going Public

To begin this discussion, let us consider which implementation actions should be taken early on to ready the corporate environment and lay the groundwork for change. Prior to any public announcements introducing valuing diversity as a long-term goal, organizations should begin building a solid foundation for change adoption by creating a broad rationale for valuing diversity, as well as by identifying planning systems and support mechanisms required to guide the overall implementation process. In particular, seven preliminary steps can be taken to help build this foundation including:

1. Selecting the core leadership team.

2. Compiling the complete business case.

3. Assessing the culture's impact.

4. Creating the project plan.

5. Crafting the vision and key start-up messages.

6. Involving the organization leadership.

7. Building broad ownership.

Selecting the Core Leadership Team

As is true of all culture change initiatives, institutionalizing the value of diversity can only be accomplished through a well-organized, comprehensive, long-term corporate effort. Because implementing this paradigm requires complex systems change and ongoing support, a core team of knowledgeable project leaders is *always required* to guide the process. Without this team in place, the chances of successful implementation would be greatly diminished; therefore, among the earliest and most important steps in implementation is selection of this core leadership team.

Ideally, this group should consist of 8 to 12 women and men—representing a wide spectrum of organizational diversity—who have demonstrated leadership capabilities, change management skills, commitment to the new paradigm, and who are also dedicated to planning and managing the overall effort. When it comes to diversity adoption, this core team should consist largely of change agents, with a few innovators and pragmatists to maximize creativity and help ground the effort in practicality.

In many organizations today, core leadership teams consist solely of senior executives and deliberately exclude people at other organizational levels. Although such executive involvement is desirable from the start of implementation, it is often unwise to use hierarchic position as the sole criterion for selecting project leaders. Highly effective core teams usually include a balance of individuals with and without formal role power who together provide the diverse perspectives and create the synergy required to succeed with culture change. Rather than make organizational position the essential qualification, it is more useful to make position on the Diversity Adoption Curve, knowledge about multicultural issues, and capacity to do the work the three main criteria for core team selection.

Core Team Responsibilities

Assuming all core team candidates meet these three criteria, there are several other abilities that this team should also possess. To effectively function as change leaders, core team members must be capable of challenging old organizational assumptions, of thinking creatively and inclusively about implementation, and of taking timely action. To accomplish their long-term goal, members must engage in candid discussion, honest inquiry, and constructive critique about the current institutional environment, while avoiding the temptation to defend whatever may not be working. In short, they must be capable and committed to addressing real organizational issues and managing long-term culture change.

Planning and leading the implementation process is often challenging and time-consuming. It requires considerable training, knowledge, and skill. While each team member may not be experienced in all aspects of change management, the group must be capable of taking responsibility for:

1. Soliciting input from a wide spectrum of sources within and outside the organization.

2. Identifying and addressing critical implementation issues.

3. Objectively analyzing facts and reaching valid, nondefensive conclusions about environmental readiness.

4. Developing specific, timely, and meaningful action plans.

5. Assigning follow-up tasks to individuals, teams, and functional groups and holding them accountable.

6. Maintaining a close, working partnership with the organization leadership on all diversity management matters.

Core Team Building and Ongoing Education

While the selection of qualified team members will not assure full adoption, this core leadership group is an essential element in the change process. In many respects, the ongoing involvement and preparedness of the core leadership team is the single most important factor in predicting implementation success. When they are skillful change leaders, knowledgeable about multicultural issues and able to work effectively together, core team members can make the essential difference. They can take the new paradigm of valuing

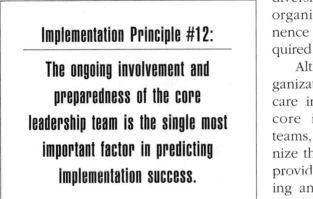

Implementation Principle #12:

The ongoing involvement and preparedness of the core leadership team is the single most important factor in predicting Implementation success.

diversity and give it the organizational prominence and support required for full adoption.

Although some organizations take great care in selecting their core implementation teams, too few recognize the importance of providing team building and ongoing education for this group after its formation. Despite the fact that there are always knowledge and skill gaps within this team, time and resources for development are often quite limited. Yet, the needs for a cohesive working relationship and an in-depth understanding of diverse human and organizational issues are enormous.

To work effectively on implementation planning, core team members must build an open, trusting relationship with each other. They must recognize the personal assumptions they each bring to the discussion of valuing diversity and move beyond these to create mutually acceptable goals. For some members, the need to build a broad knowledge of multicultural issues is often enormous. For others, a deeper understanding of the principles of change adoption and implementation management is required. Before the basic work of data gathering can even begin, these needs for team building and basic literacy education must first be addressed. In addition, to remain effective throughout the implementation process, this core team must also commit to continuing education and development. As such, they must be willing to invest in themselves as a group in order to model cohesive, cross-cultural interaction for others in their organization. In institutions where valuing diversity is understood to be a long-term culture change, the importance of educating and building common ground within this core leadership team is taken very seriously.

Compiling the Complete Business Case

Once all core team leaders are in place, their first priority should then be building a complete business case for valuing diversity. Because most employees will want to know the why behind valuing diversity, a well-articulated, specific business case is extremely important. Minimally, this description of diversity's strategic importance should address the following:

Employment marketplace issues: How changes in the labor force impact recruitment, hiring, and retention in the organization.

Competitive issues: How changing customer demographics and demands impact the business and its operation. Benchmarking what the competition is doing to meet diverse customer needs.

Current costs of not valuing diversity: A review of attrition patterns; employee discrimination complaints and lawsuit settlements; exit interview feedback; employee opinion survey data and other relevant morale metrics; cultural assessment data; customer service feedback, including complaints; downward trends in market share; and so on.

Internal success stories of diversity in action: A review of internal examples, where valuing diversity is enhancing creative problem-solving, innovation, and break-through thinking; examples of the positive impact of valuing diversity on employee recruitment, retention, morale, and so on. External examples of enhanced customer service, increased market share, reduced service complaints, and so forth, that resulted from this paradigm shift.

External success stories of diversity in action: A review of competitor and industry examples, where valuing diversity has built market share and enhanced customer satisfaction, employee morale, innovation, productivity, and profitability.

Assessing the Culture's Impact

To help identify environmental issues that adversely impact diverse groups and may impede adoption, organizations usually conduct an internal assessment of employee attitudes at the start of implementation. Such assessments will range from very elaborate (with hundreds of employees participating in individual interviews, written survey feedback, and focus group discussions) to less complicated data-gathering procedures aimed at understanding the impact of the corporate culture on diverse employee groups and clients/customers. Based on an issue analysis of the data gathered, it is then possible to begin building a project plan to address barriers in the environment that are widely perceived by employees to be impeding change adoption.

In many organizations, where employee opinion surveys about the organization climate have been conducted for many years, there is often an attempt to tie the results of this general survey to readiness to value diversity. However, since most of these general opinion surveys were developed with other goals in mind, their results do not easily translate into meaningful data about organizational readiness to value diversity. Rather than attempt to use an existing but inaccurate measure to build the case for culture change, it is much wiser to construct a new survey. This specific, written instrument can then be used to gather opinions and validate key issues identified in group and individual interviews. As such, it becomes a supporting piece of the data-gathering process, as opposed to being the sole measure of organizational readiness.

While some would argue that a very large sample of respondents is required to truly understand an organization culture's impact on diversity, such grandiose efforts often lead to data overload, considerable expense, and few new insights about conditions in the environment. Prolonged data gathering can also result in unnecessary delays in the implementation process and may cause the effort to remain trapped in this preliminary stage for months or, in some cases, even years.

In truth, cultural assessments need not be grandiose or cumbersome to be effective. In most cases, a small, diverse sample of employees, former employees, and client/customers can yield the critical data required to help set priorities and guide the change process. When there is doubt about the need for a large employee sample, experience in many organizations would suggest that a smaller sample and more in-depth data-gathering techniques often yield equally accurate and more user-friendly results. However, regardless of the optimal sample size, the help of experienced researchers can often be useful in designing questionnaires, conducting confidential interviews, and analyzing results.

Creating the Project Plan

Once all data-gathering steps have been completed and the most critical issues identified, it is time to begin developing a multiyear follow-up plan. This project plan should include a description of specific programs and actions that will be initiated to accelerate adoption as well as a time line for their introduction. Accountabilities should also be assigned and measurable outcomes identified for each follow-up step. Because some later steps in a five-year implementation plan will evolve out of early follow-up actions, it will be impossible to identify all of these at this stage. However, it is reasonable to expect that capital and human resources will be required for continuous follow-up and to begin identifying funding needs for early, interim, and long-term actions.

Because adoption of the value of diversity requires comprehensive changes in the assumptions, beliefs, systems, and practices of an organization, implementation is often a complex process to understand and manage. As particular changes are introduced into the environment, their ripple effects create new, unanticipated issues and opportunities. These, in turn, lead to other adjustments in project direction, assumptions, systems, practices, and so on.

As the overall change process evolves over many months and years, it is important for the implementation team to recognize that this initial project plan must also evolve. No matter how careful the initial planning, it is simply not possible to precisely predict the future. Rather than attempt to anticipate all that will be required for full adoption at the start of implementation, it is far more practical to focus on those high-leverage actions that will be taken in the first two years of implementation and then to broadly outline what else is likely to follow.

Crafting the Vision and Key Start-Up Messages

Based on the specific business case that has been developed for the organization, a long-term vision statement should now be developed to set the overall direction for the effort. While such statements have become hackneyed in many organizations because of overabundance and lack of real-world relevance, a thoughtful vision statement can also become a useful measure of real progress over time. To be of use, this statement should provide a definition of diversity and describe what the organizational culture will be like when diversity is understood, respected, and fully leveraged.

Creating this statement can be an important step in the implementation process. When organization leaders and employees at many levels help to build this vision, it can become an important collective perspective that represents shared hopes, needs, and common values. To be perceived as a shared vision of the future, this statement must include the hopes and goals of many diverse constituencies and be developed using an interactive, inclusive process.

After this long-term vision is crafted, a set of key communications must then be created to introduce the change process within the organization. Among the analogies and descriptions that many organizations have used, five stand out as particularly reassuring and appropriate in this start-up phase. Together, these key themes describe what the change implementation process will be like. They help to set expectations and acknowledge the long-term nature of the change process. Finally, they emphasize the common needs that people have for respect and inclusion. Here are five useful themes that can be used effectively to help set the stage for change:

1. We want to create an environment where everyone is respected and included.

2. We also want to leverage our diversity for competitive advantage.

3. Accomplishing this will require changing some assumptions, practices, and beliefs as an organization.

4. These changes will not happen quickly or be done recklessly.

5. As our culture evolves, we will need to work together to make our diversity work for us.

Involving the Organization Leadership

Early in this chapter, we discussed the danger of selecting the core leadership team based solely on organizational level. While many within the formal leadership group may not be ready for this core planning role, there is another important role for those leaders who are most receptive to change (i.e., the innovators, change agents, and, hopefully, some pragmatists). This part is as spokesperson to the organization at large. Leaders in these segments can become visible communicators of the corporate vision, key start-up messages, and specific business benefits of valuing diversity.

While executive change agents can sometimes be relied on to do more than this, in most organizations their numbers will be few at best. Nonetheless, in a few companies like Avon Products and Levis Strauss & Company, the president and CEO have chosen to play a very active part in diversity implementation by enthusiastically initiating and engaging in ongoing dialogue and co-facilitating awareness training sessions for other employees.

Executive Education

Sometimes special awareness training that focuses on prejudice reduction may be done to help prepare organization leaders for implementation. While such training is likely to be viewed as useful by change agents and some innovators, it is less likely to help pragmatists, skeptics, and traditionalists. The more executive education focuses on the business case for valuing diversity, the more likely it is that pragmatists will regard it as useful. In addition, a strong element of peer interaction and peer support for diversity must be included in the seminar design in order to reach this segment.

As for skeptics and traditionalists, while organizational protocol may dictate that they be included in early executive education sessions, they are unlikely to benefit from awareness-building activities. Before they buy in, they will require compelling evidence that their peers and the hierarchy support this change—evidence that will need to accumulate over a considerable period of time.

Because their role as organizational leaders often demands that skeptics and traditionalists behave like pragmatists and not openly oppose change, it is helpful to think in these terms when educating and coaching leaders from these segments. By describing the value of diversity in pragmatic business terms, providing a specific script for introducing the new paradigm and coaching individuals to respond appropriately to employee questions, some skeptics and traditionalists can begin to act the part of the pragmatist. However, while they may be required to talk supportively about the new paradigm, their early communications are likely to be regarded as "performances" by those with whom they speak. Until they perceive valuing diversity as a mainstream reality and recognize some personal benefits in adoption, the most they can be expected to do is pay lip service to diversity rather than truly adopt this change.

Building Broad Ownership

In preparation for the public announcement of diversity implementation, it is also appropriate to begin taking actions to involve the organizational mainstream in this change process. As we have already discussed, involvement of white men and all other core identity groups in the organization is an absolute must—if full adoption of diversity is to occur. By emphasizing that this new paradigm is inclusive of everyone and by using a multidimensional definition of diversity, change leaders can help assure employees that no one group or groups will be left out. Their early emphasis on inclusion and mutual respect can also help to defuse cynicism about the alleged "real intent" behind this change, making it more difficult for resistance and backlash to build. While some suspicions about the new paradigm are likely to remain until more proof is available, continued assurances from the change leaders that there is a place at the table for everyone can help reduce employee resistance and accelerate adoption.

Thinking Globally . . . Acting Locally

Another element of broad ownership has to do with globalization of the valuing diversity change process. While most institutional efforts to value diversity begin as U.S.-focused initiatives, many are evolving into global efforts in multinational organizations. Since this paradigm shift is being driven in part by legislative and social changes within the United States, it is naive to presume that the philosophy of valuing diversity can be exported without some major modifications. Adoption of the value of diversity cannot happen in a vacuum. Before this change can be adopted, societal and institutional values must first be in alignment.

In many countries, valuing diversity has yet to be recognized as a desirable goal. As such, it remains an alien concept with no real societal support. How can global organizations build ownership for an alien idea that is not supported in the larger culture or society? Building broad ownership for this paradigm demands highly flexible implementation. This flexible implementation must take into account the diversity in cultural norms and expectations that exists across countries. It cannot presume that a one-size-fits-all approach to implementation will work or that adoption of this change will result in similar outcomes throughout the global organization.

To be effective (as opposed to disruptive) in diverse cultures, corporate efforts must be modified based on conditions in each local environment. By encouraging communication across diverse regions, those who manage the change process can benefit from the global insights and experiences of all other organizational groups; in effect, they can think globally about diversity and then modify ideas in order to act locally. To build acceptance of the new paradigm, each country implementation team must ultimately create a plan that supports the broad organizational goals of inclusion and respect, while recognizing and adapting to local conditions and cultural norms.

In this chapter, we have reviewed key actions that must be taken to ready the environment and set the stage so adoption can begin.

While there is always a temptation to "just get on with it," there are no shortcuts when it comes to implementing diversity. Careful, up-front planning is a critical prerequisite for long-term success. By investing time and resources to lay the groundwork before going public with this change, all follow-up efforts can then be linked to the long-term vision and introduced in a logical context. Instead of appearing to be random activities, their tie-in to the organization culture change can now be easily understood. As a result, communications, education, and systems changes are now seen as parts of a coherent whole—an exciting, long-term change process that promises benefit for employees and customers and renewal for the organization.

FOURTEEN

Reaching the Segments

While recognition of the five distinctly different segments on the Diversity Adoption Curve is a giant step towards designing a successful implementation plan, it is obviously not enough. Along with recognition, managers and implementers must understand how to reach all segments and address their diverse concerns and needs. To achieve full adoption, all communications, education, and follow-up involvement in the change process must be designed with different segments in mind. The following case history illustrates just how critical this multitiered approach can be and what often happens when it is not recognized by an organization's core implementation team.

IF ELECTED . . . I WILL NOT SERVE

Harry M., a traditionalist, is a senior executive with a large aerospace company who reports directly to the CEO. He manages a technical support division of 4,000+ employees, approximately 80 percent of whom are men. Harry is an engineer by training. He attended an all-male university. During his 30+ year career, he has never worked for a woman.

Currently, all eight managers who report to Harry are men. While he states that he is not opposed to having more women in management, Harry also believes that no women engineers meet the qualifications for appointment to a senior position in his division. (While the majority of his direct reports agree with this assessment, there are a minority who believe otherwise.)

In order to help identify and develop women for visible leadership roles, Harry's company recently instituted a senior management mentoring program. As part of this developmental effort, every division manager in the company is now required to serve as a mentor/informal coach to two women managers with "high potential."

137

Harry thinks this program and the "preferential treatment" it provides is bad for the company. While he spoke out strongly against the mentoring initiative when it was first proposed, he was unable to influence his boss. The CEO is strongly behind the mentoring plan and has made it clear that everyone on the executive team must get behind it, too.

Since then, Harry has found himself increasingly isolated when the subject of mentoring comes up. While he knows that some of his peers agree with him, he is now the "only one in the cabinet who is telling the truth and not being politically correct."

Harry resents the fact that this mentoring initiative is taking up so much of his time. He has told his secretary, "We have pressing, bottom-line business issues, and here I am baby-sitting two women!" He is also concerned about "the potential for a harassment complaint" that the program invites. To protect himself, he has insisted that the women he is coaching both be present for each of their meetings.

Since the mentoring initiative started five months ago, Harry has met with his two protégées on three occasions. At the start of each meeting, he always asks if there are any questions about "what it takes to succeed around here." Then he moves on and offers some of his perspectives about effective leadership. In their last meeting, he stressed "the importance of tough, aggressive leadership" and the need for "a commanding presence that demands respect from the troops." While Harry had hoped that these thoughts would stimulate some response from the two women, they reacted in a manner that he perceived as "passive and disinterested."

This afternoon, Harry received a visit from his boss. It seems Harry's two protégées have requested a new mentor. Upon hearing this news, Harry's boss was very concerned. As he discussed the situation with his boss, Harry attempted to explain how he was conducting each meeting, but the CEO wasn't interested. Instead, he looked at Harry and said, "Why do you insist on being the dinosaur, Harry? This is a project that's important to the company and to me. From this point forward, I don't want anymore complaints or excuses. I just want you to make it work!" Then the meeting ended.

Frustrated and confused, Harry now feels more isolated and trapped in a situation he can't seem to successfully resolve. Reflecting on the CEO's comments, Harry muses, "This is an unfair rap!

I've done my best to work with those two women—regardless of what they're saying to my boss. I don't know what else they want from me!"

Key Questions:

1. Assuming this is the second year of implementation, which segment(s) of the organization are most ready to serve as mentors?
2. Is the decision to make executive participation mandatory likely to enhance the effectiveness of this program?
3. What else could be done to help prepare Harry and other traditionalists for this change?

While it is difficult to convince people who are enthusiastic about this change that others may not yet be ready for adoption, the fact remains that *this is always so* in the early stages of diversity implementation. Unfortunately, premature involvement of a segment before a level of readiness is reached often backfires. Not only does it derail many worthy initiatives, it also increases confusion and fear among those who are not yet ready.

Differences in Readiness

In the early stages of implementation, when the majority of people in an organization appear disinterested or opposed to change, it is tempting to push them into greater active involvement. When this produces a less-than-desirable response from skeptics and traditionalists, it is then tempting to categorize these segments as difficult people or "dinosaurs." However, making "them and their negative attitudes" the problem, does little to speed adoption of change. In fact, it often does just the opposite.

To succeed with diversity adoption, organizations must be able to recognize and respond appropriately to differences in segment readiness. Rather than think in terms of a single approach to communication, education, follow-up involvement, and so on, core implementers must think in terms of five progressive paths to change—one each for innovators, change agents, pragmatists, skeptics, and traditionalists. While all five paths should be built around a common set of goals, they will each vary in terms of required time frames and appropriate activities. As each segment embarks on its own path towards adoption, committed managers and diversity implementers must be available to join them on the journey— providing appropriate levels of guidance, information, challenge, and support along the way.

Segment Predispositions

Whether we are about to try a new flavor of ice cream, buy a car, or consider a new paradigm for working with others, each of us starts out more positively or negatively predisposed to new ideas and experiences. These early inclinations to be open or closed to change vary depending upon the level of perceived risk that we associate with a particular change. Our predispositions toward change influence our overt reactions. They motivate us to get more involved, keep our distance, or retreat. When it comes to valuing diversity, every segment on the Diversity Adoption Curve starts out with a more positive or negative predisposition towards this change. No two segments share the exact same predisposition. Depending upon how effectively a segment's needs and concerns are addressed throughout implementation, these predispositions or inclinations will be reinforced or modified. Therefore, creating an implementation plan that reinforces and builds on the positive predispositions of innovators and change agents while modifying the negative predispositions of other segments is the ultimate challenge facing managers and implementers of diversity.

Among **innovators,** where predisposition is the most positive, there will be little or no need to defuse objections to this change or overcome resistance to the idea of valuing diversity. Instead, innovators will be looking for greater opportunities to experiment and create. They will be interested in discovering better ways to leverage diversity. While they may be interested in exploring what is being done in other leading-edge organizations, they will have less interest in what is happening in their own; for, as innovators, they will be ahead of the curve and already beyond where the organization is ready to go. In some cases, it may even become necessary to reign in the innovators' desire to modify and continue changing the new paradigm. To prevent runaway modifications, it may be useful to provide this segment with a mechanism for continued experimentation with the valuing diversity paradigm under controlled conditions.

While **change agents** perceive risk associated with creating innovation and being out in front of the curve, they like to be among the first to try out the best of the new ideas discovered or developed by the innovators. As such, their predisposition to valuing diversity will be largely positive—once they recognize the potential benefits of the new paradigm. Within this group, there will be a strong need to know more about the genesis of this change and its impact on people, about the dimensions of diversity, as well as organizational issues, opportunities, and best practices for successful implementation. Because change agents are eager to learn more about diversity, it is important that they have easy access to in-depth information from the start of implementation. Books and other readings, films, discussion groups, seminars, workshops, and so forth, will all be welcomed and are likely to be deemed very useful by most members of this group. In addition to increasing awareness, this information should begin to answer change agents' questions about the how-to's of diversity implementation; for this segment will be most favorably predisposed to trying out new ideas, piloting new programs, and leading the overall effort.

Among **pragmatists,** where some suspicions about the practicality of this change exist, there will a predisposition to wait rather than move quickly towards full adoption. In order to help this segment progress from waiting to adopting, quantitative evidence to support the business case for diversity will be required. In addition, within this segment there will be strong interest in business case histories, live examples of diversity's demonstrated value inside the organization, and curiosity about early and successful efforts of change agent colleagues to value diversity. Because pragmatists will want to simplify rather than delve into the complexities of diversity issues and opportunities, they will be most interested in practical, how-to training that will help them deal with "real-world" implementation problems and less interested in education that is aimed at increasing their sensitivity to intercultural issues and heightening personal awareness.

Among **skeptics,** there will be a predisposition to delay implementation of this change as long as possible. Among traditionalists, the most negatively predisposed segment, there will be a tendency to avoid involvement totally. Within both segments, strong resistance to this change and considerable challenging will be likely at the start of implementation. In organizations where skeptics and traditionalists are empowered to speak out and act on their views, it is likely that members of both segments will boycott all awareness training, as well as other communication and educational efforts aimed at building early organizational support for change.

Rather than actively involve **skeptics** or **traditionalists** in core leadership teams, awareness training, design of systems changes, and so on, these segments should be targeted for clear, consistent, ongoing communication about the organization's commitment to change adoption, the benefits that valuing diversity offers the organization, and the importance of acquiring competencies to work effectively with *others*. Ongoing public endorsements of the value of diversity by organizational leaders is a particularly useful strategy for reaching skeptics. In addition, as implementation gets under way, behavior-based skills training to help individuals develop the communications and interpersonal skills required to interact effectively with *others* and, therefore, meet new organizational requirements for continued employment and success will also be appropriate for many skeptics and some traditionalists. While out of favor with some supporters of self-empowerment philosophies, authoritarianism is often a useful perspective to employ when designing programs to reach skeptics and traditionalists. When administered with a careful hand, a dose of "here's what you should do and how you should do it," from those in authority will often have the greatest impact on these segments' interest in adopting change.

Key Segment Variables

Because of differences in predisposition towards change, each segment on the Diversity Adoption Curve requires a customized menu of communications, education, initial involvement, and follow-up reinforcement to achieve the goal of full adoption. To accelerate adoption across all segments of the organization and minimize backlash, each menu must take into account and be designed around several important variables, including:

Level of perceived risk: The extent to which a segment perceives valuing diversity as a potential threat.

Primary motivation: The principal reason(s) why a segment would be interested in adopting the value of diversity.

Key segment messages: Major themes to emphasize in communications to a particular segment.

Timing of segment involvement: The appropriate time for involving a particular segment in the implementation process.

Level of Perceived Risk

As we discussed in Chapter 6, every segment perceives valuing diversity in terms of risk and opportunity. While **innovators** tend to focus almost exclusively on the potential opportunities, as one moves farther towards the right on the Diversity Adoption Curve, the level of perceived risk associated with this change increases. Recognizing the degree to which valuing diversity is perceived to be a threat or an opportunity is important when targeting segments, for this perception will shape how early and how actively a particular segment will want to be involved in implementation.

Among **change agents,** information about the potential benefits that valuing diversity offers to people and the organization is welcomed at the start of implementation. Once the human case for change is clear, this group is ready to become actively involved in implementation. In the early stages of implementation, most change agents will be interested in learning more about diversity—both the issues that surround it and the opportunities that adoption offers. For **pragmatists,** a strong business case that spells out the economic benefits of valuing diversity can help to diminish perceived risk. In addition, endorsements from change agents who have successfully leveraged diversity for competitive advantage will also help reinforce the fact that valuing diversity has a proven record of success and offers practical business benefits.

For **skeptics,** perceived risk is likely to remain high for a considerable period of time after diversity implementation begins. While innovators, change agents, and even some pragmatists may adopt this change within the first two years of implementation, it can often be several more years before most skeptics are ready to accept this change. However, over time, as diversity's strategic importance continues to grow in the organization and the majority of leaders strongly endorse this value, most skeptics will be persuaded that this change is not a fad but, instead, is becoming a permanent part of the organizational fabric. At this point, the perception of risk will begin to diminish, and pressure to remain part of the organization majority and adopt this institutional reality will increase. Does this mean that skeptics eventually become change agents or innovators as their perceptions of risk diminish over time? Definitely not. Instead, some skeptics are likely to join the pragmatists in their support of the value of diversity as a mainstream business imperative. Once they are convinced that valuing diversity is an irreversible, corporate reality, skeptics *will* buy in.

Finally, while some **traditionalists** will never overcome their fears and adopt this change, others will be motivated to get on board with valuing diversity rather than risk being left on the platform as the caboose of the organizational train leaves the station. Once valuing diversity becomes an institutionalized standard, traditionalists face the choice of either adopting this change or dealing with the consequences of lagging behind. As the negative consequences of not adopting change increase, traditionalists often find themselves rethinking their earlier predisposition. Instead of working to avoid this change, they now want to avoid the negative consequences of *not* changing.

When the consequences of adopting the value of diversity are perceived as less threatening than the consequences of not adopting this paradigm, many traditionalists will begin to view adoption as the more appealing alternative. Linking valuing diversity to recognition, rewards, and compensation is one way of reinforcing the positive consequences of adoption. Upward feedback from peers and employees can also be useful in efforts to reinforce the importance of valuing diversity and the consequences to individuals of being seen as effective and less effective.

Motivation

Just as levels of perceived risk vary across segments, so do the basic drives that impel segments to adopt change. Among most **innovators,** the promise of creative fulfillment and increased innovation motivate adoption of the value of diversity; for at its core, this is the greatest single benefit that the new paradigm offers. Among **change agents,** valuing diversity is often viewed as an opportunity to enhance personal knowledge; promote inclusion, respect, and cooperation; and, increase one's organizational influence and stature. As such, the most powerful motivators for change agent adoption include the desire for social leadership, enhanced knowledge, and the opportunity to help others.

While **pragmatists** will wait for innovators and change agents to test out and refine an idea before they consider adoption, they also desire acceptance and approval from these segments. When their more progressive colleagues begin to experience success as a result of valuing diversity, pragmatists become more interested in adoption. They now begin to see this change as less risky and more practical. What's more, it also represents a way to gain approval from their innovator and change agent peers.

Because **skeptics** see significant risks associated with adoption, they use considerable energy to resist this change. During the early stages of implementation, they may be joined by pragmatists, who have yet to be convinced of the economic benefits of this change. At this point, many skeptics will feel confident that they are part of the more informed majority who reject the value of diversity. However, as their pragmatic peers begin to adopt this change and their organizational leaders continue to insist that it is not going away, skeptics start to notice that they are losing majority support for their position. Objecting to change was fine when there were many other voices joining them, since belonging is a strong motivation for this group. But skeptics are reluctant to continue playing the contrarian role once they believe that the majority of their peers and leaders support adoption and the organization is behind it.

Traditionalists, on the other hand, will often continue to resist change even after the majority of their peers have adopted it. Only when traditionalists see their own success (or failure) directly tied to their ability to value diversity will they begin to adopt this change. At the point in implementation when consequences shift and it becomes more painful to resist than to adopt the value of diversity, traditionalists will begin to consider adoption. However, because many members of this segment have serious skill deficiencies that will impede successful adoption, their increased desire to adopt change must now be paired with skill development, coaching, and ongoing feedback.

Key Segment Communications

Because primary motivations for adoption differ across segments, a comprehensive communication program must include targeted messages that appeal to each category. For **innovators,** communication must emphasize the potential that valuing diversity offers for enhanced creativity, more effective team relations and, therefore, continuous improvement in results. **Change agents** will be most interested in communications that emphasize self-learning, the benefits that valuing diversity offers to all employees, and the important difference that one can make by leading this change effort.

Pragmatists, who are likely to be suspicious of this change if it is presented as something that is only "good for people," will respond more favorably to communications about the business case for valuing diversity. A strong good-for-business argument and successful examples of valuing diversity in action are the principal themes that should be emphasized in communications targeted to this segment.

While it is tempting to assume that **skeptics** will also respond to the business case for diversity, this is simply not so in the early stages of implementation. Because they fear the consequences of adopting this change, skeptics will reject social *and* bottom-line arguments that support the value of diversity; however, they will be less likely to continue challenging the appropriateness of this change when their leaders come forward to actively support it. In addition, while they will resist early adoption, later in the implementation process skeptics will be motivated by communications that imply that their continued resistance to change is beginning to be out of synch with mainstream values.

Finally, for **traditionalists,** communication must include ongoing repetitive endorsements from organizational leaders about the strategic importance of valuing diversity and emphasis on adoption as a more productive, less painful alternative to continued resistance. While it may seem to the reader that this is not a compelling enough argument for change, it is the one that is most likely to capture the interest of traditionalists when it is repeated often over a period of several years and linked to other traditional and respected values such as pulling together, loyalty, commitment to the organization, and so on. Unlike innovators and change agents, who find the newness of change appealing, with traditionalists, it is unwise to emphasize this aspect of valuing diversity. Instead, making this idea seem more like an extension of traditional values and norms is a better way to position the value of diversity with this segment.

Different Message Biases

While valuing diversity is a single idea, it does not appeal to everyone at the same time in the same way. Each segment on the Diversity Adoption Curve has particular biases about change that can help increase interest in adoption. **Innovators** respond with enthusiasm to messages emphasizing personal benefit and promising new solutions to complex problems. **Change agents** respond most readily to utilitarian messages that offer potential improvement for self and others. **Pragmatists** like proof messages and, in particular, respond well to examples of the success of change agents. **Skeptics** respond best to proof messages as well. In addition to change agent success stories, they want majority proof, expert endorsements, and industry proof. **Traditionalists** respond best to authoritarian messages, as well as to messages that offer security and stability.

In communicating to different segments, messages should vary. They should be constructed to appeal to particular segment biases about the potential benefits of adoption. Construction of a message should also take into account the fact that an ideal appeal for one segment may be a disaster when used with another. For example, the excitement of change will be an enticement for innovators, but this same message will be a repellent to skeptics and traditionalists. In creating communications targeted at all groups, it is important to present a variety of benefits in order to assure that each segment is able to consider the one(s) that it finds particularly appealing.

Timing of Segment Involvement

No two segments on the adoption curve heed the same call to value diversity nor do they heed the particular messages that appeal to them at the same point in time. The farther to the right one is on the Diversity Adoption Curve, the longer it will take before readiness to actively engage in the change process occurs. This is not just because of the higher perceived level of risk associated with change. It is also due to the time required to build strong support for change in the preceding segments. Beyond the **innovator** and **change agent** segments, all other segments to the right on the Diversity Adoption Curve require strong peer and authority endorsements before adopting change. Since such endorsements are never in evidence at the start of implementation, they must be built up over time. Then, like a domino effect, the strength of commitment to the change and increasing adoption in one segment will begin to influence the attitudes of those in the next segment to the right on the curve.

In order to persuade **pragmatists** to value diversity, one must first persuade change agents to adopt the new paradigm. In order to convince skeptics, one must first assure that pragmatists buy in, thus tilting majority opinion towards adoption of change and away from continued resistance. In every segment, there is a need for proof of value, and this proof can only be supplied by those peers and authority figures in the preceding segment(s) who have already chosen to adopt change.

While timing of involvement will vary across segments, this does not mean that **pragmatists, skeptics,** and **traditionalists** should be completely left out of early efforts to communicate and announce implementation. On the contrary, total exclusion would only heighten fear and resistance in these groups. Instead, a base-line level of communication should be directed at all groups throughout implementation in order to assure that all segments realize valuing diversity is coming. However, while general communications mechanisms such as company meetings and employee newsletters may be used to announce the coming change to everyone, active engagement in planning, training, and other support activities should occur segment-by-segment.

The following chart contrasts the predispositions, levels of perceived risk, motivations, and key communications that should be used in overall implementation planning. While education is another critical variable that must also be considered when attempting to reach each segment, it is not discussed here. Instead, it will be reviewed separately in Chapter 15.

REACHING THE SEGMENTS: KEY VARIABLES

Variables	Innovators	Change Agents	Pragmatists	Skeptics	Traditionalists
Segment predispositions:	Want to experiment and create	Want to try early	Want to wait initially	Want to delay	Want to avoid entirely
Levels of perceived risk:	Lowest	Low	Moderate	High	Highest
Primary motivations for adoption:	Increased innovation	Status, self-knowledge, helping others	Economic benefit and peer acceptance	Authority endorsement and majority inclusion	Reduced discomfort and meeting revised organization standards
Key messages for segment communications:	It enhances innovation and leads to continuous improvement.	You can make a difference by leading this change. It's good for all people. It's knowledge-enhancing.	It's good for business. It's a proven success. Adoption will enhance your standing with peers.	It's supported by organization leaders. If you don't adopt, you'll be left behind.	It's now an organization standard. To succeed, you need to adopt this change.

Involving the Change Agents Early

As we have already discussed, early involvement of change agents is key to successful adoption of the value of diversity in every organization. Because change agents influence pragmatists and shape public opinion about change, it is important to actively engage them at every organizational level in implementation efforts. Culturally diverse, multilevel change agents can be effective role models, mentors, and spokespersons for the value of diversity. They can help educate their peers, build broad support for change, and maintain momentum for adoption over several years.

Regardless of their diverse backgrounds, most change agents still need to acquire some new skills, increased awareness, and an understanding of change adoption to be truly effective as role models, mentors, and live witnesses for the value of diversity. Despite the fact that developing awareness and skills takes time, there is no segment more open to learning, investing, and spreading the news about the benefits that valuing diversity offers than this one. Therefore, during the first year of implementation, it is this

segment that should be targeted for education and early involvement if full adoption is the long-term organization goal.

Influencing the Majority

While direct, early involvement of change agents is essential during
the first year of implementation, it is equally important to avoid
involving pragmatists and skeptics in the same manner. To convince
pragmatists of the importance of adoption, a strong business case
must first be developed. The costs of not valuing diversity must be
quantified and the potential economic impact of change adoption
must also be identified.

After analyzing the business case, pragmatists will then be ready
to hear from their change agent peers about the successes they are
having with the new paradigm. Rather than attempt to convince
them of the importance of this change *before* a thorough case has
been researched and developed, it will be important to gather
economic evidence and organizational examples first and build the
case before involving this segment. To paraphrase a now-famous
line from a recent movie, "Once you build it, the pragmatists will
come!"

As the pragmatist segment warms to the idea of adoption, many
skeptics will begin to sense that they are becoming more isolated
in their continued resistance to change. When the organization's
systems and practices begin to change and rewards are linked more
directly to valuing diversity, most skeptics will finally see that they
are now swimming against a strong organizational tide. Rather than
exhaust themselves and risk drowning, this segment will begin to
adopt change, even as they continue to listen hopefully for signs
of wavering commitment from their organizational leaders. Finally,
several years after implementation begins, skeptics will be persuaded to adopt change; however, most will then require considerable coaching, education, and behavior change in order to be
effective as diversity leaders, managers, and so on.

Managing the Traditionalists

While valuing diversity is a fundamental paradigm shift, it is not a
mindset change that most traditionalists can be expected to make
for many years, if ever. Fear of this change is simply too powerful

for some individuals to overcome. However, although changing one's mindset may not always be possible, changing one's behavior is. By defining clear and specific parameters of acceptable and unacceptable behavior, it is possible to effect behavior changes among traditionalists that support the value of diversity. In so doing, traditionalists can begin to act more consistently and appropriately, even though the risk that they associate with this change remains relatively high.

Over time, as many traditionalists become more comfortable "acting the part," perceived risk will likely diminish. Although not destined to become change agents, who enthusiastically encourage adoption, traditionalists can make a successful transition from adamantly resisting change to supporting it through their behavior. Once they succeed at changing their behavior and increase their own comfort dealing with diversity, mindset change will be more likely to follow.

Implementation Principle #13:

Not only will adoption be more likely to occur as a result of segmentation, it will also happen more quickly, with less confusion and less conflict.

Although it is easier to design a single plan for encouraging adoption of change, it is not possible to do so and effectively reach all segments. Segment differences in predisposition and perceived risk preclude this possibility from working effectively. By customizing communications and segment involvement based on differences in perceived risk and motivation to change, managers and diversity implementers can avoid many of the classic mistakes that have been outlined in this book and assure full adoption of the value of diversity.

Attending to the specific concerns and motivations of each segment makes real change possible. With a customized implementation plan that builds on the enthusiasm and good will of innovators and change agents, pragmatists can be turned into supporters. As this occurs, skeptics begin to take notice of the increased momentum building in support of change. Once they are certain that their leaders support it, they, too, will embrace the new paradigm. Eventually, several years after implementation begins, many traditionalists will finally recognize this change as the new organizational reality and buy in.

Although not widely practiced in organizations, a segmented approach to implementation can make the ultimate difference between success and failure; for segmentation provides important insights into the ways people perceive the valuing diversity paradigm and their readiness to adopt it. Rather than force all employees into the deep end of the pool regardless of whether they can swim or not, segmenting the organization can help us appreciate and address diverse levels of interest, ability, understanding, and need throughout all phases of implementation. Not only will adoption be more likely to occur as a result, it will also happen more quickly, with less confusion and less conflict. Considering the proven risks associated with ignoring these differences, why would one consider anything other than a segmented approach to implementation now?

FIFTEEN

The Diversity Curriculum

While awareness of cultural diversity is increasing in our society, most people still have limited exposure to many cultures and limited consciousness regarding the predictable dynamics that occur when diverse people interact. Because few of us are well prepared by our life experiences to truly value diversity, we often have difficulty doing this competently when it becomes a job requirement. Instead, the gaps in our understanding, experience, empathy, and skillset often cause us to do a less-than-effective job. When this happens, we may experience feelings of uncertainty, confusion, embarrassment, anger, suspicion, and even fear. To overcome these emotional obstacles and acquire the knowledge needed to competently interact in, manage, and lead diverse organizations, most people require some combination of multicultural education, skill training, and coaching.

But, specifically, what do people need to learn more about and when and how should they learn it? As we have already briefly discussed, the answer depends on which segment on the Diversity Adoption Curve you are referring to. In this chapter, we will outline and discuss the key components of a basic diversity curriculum that can meet most of the awareness and skill needs of each segment on the curve and, in so doing, accelerate adoption of change.

How Much Diversity Education Is Enough?

Given the breadth and depth of information about diversity that exists on our planet, it would be virtually impossible to learn everything there is to know about all cultures and all dimensions of diversity. In addition, given what we already know about segment predispositions, it is also unrealistic to expect pragmatists, skeptics, and traditionalists to be interested in in-depth multicultural education. They simply are not and, by and large, never will be.

Nonetheless, while change agents may be the only segment interested in learning everything there is to know about diversity, the other four segments also have some distinct educational needs.

To become competent at interacting in and managing diverse work groups, most people *do* need some training. While it is tempting to offer all employees a large menu of educational offerings to meet these needs, it is unlikely that the majority will return to the buffet table more than once or twice. Therefore, deciding what to offer to each segment (content) and when to offer it (timing) are both critical decisions in building a basic diversity curriculum.

Need for Awareness and Skill Training

Today, one of the more daunting aspects of developing a diversity curriculum is choosing from the many options available in the training marketplace. In terms of content and format, the products range from more cerebral programs on intercultural etiquette and communications, all the way to highly experiential, multiday, prejudice-reduction workshops and dialogue groups that meet monthly over several years. While the proponents of each type of program tend to believe that theirs is the most useful education or training for everyone, in truth, a combination of personal awareness education, business awareness, and skills training is usually required to prepare people across all segments for change.

In creating a comprehensive menu that meets learning needs in all segments, it is important to balance personal awareness training and business awareness with skill training. In combination, these three types of diversity education can address the attitudinal, informational, and skill needs of the majority of employees. Since the variety of diversity training programs available today is enormous and often confusing, this chapter provides a brief description of the most widely utilized approaches.

Personal-Awareness Training

Personal-awareness training attempts to enlarge an individual's understanding of diversity issues. Through interactive exercises and group discussions, participants examine how their own diversity has influenced their values, beliefs, expectations, and behavior. In addition, participants explore the distinct social experiences of *others* in group-on-group discussions, videos, role plays, and so on. One common goal of personal awareness training is increased cross-cultural empathy and understanding; another is prejudice reduction. All personal awareness training is built on a strong assumption that as people hear about the lives and the diversity-related concerns of *others* in a safe and open setting, they will also increase their own empathy and understanding. This increased awareness then helps individuals interact more effectively with *others* back in the workplace.

While personal-awareness training is appropriate for less than 20 percent of an organization at the start of implementation, it is nonetheless the largest part of many corporate diversity initiatives. Over the last 20 years, many varieties of personal-awareness training have been developed in an attempt to build support for change among employees; however, while the formats may vary, the general goals have remained the same. Here is a sample of some of the more popular methods now in use:

Basic literacy workshops: Usually a one- to two-day workshop experience with a focus on prejudice reduction and, minimally, an exploration of gender and racial dynamics in the workplace. Some programs also attempt to explore how all six core dimensions of diversity shape peoples' values, assumptions, expectations, and behavior.

Dimension-specific workshops: Generally, one to two days of interactive exercises and discussion focusing on a particular dimension of diversity (e.g., gender, race, physical ability, sexual orientation, etc.), the prejudices associated with this dimension, and their impact on individuals and subgroups in the workplace and the marketplace.

Efficacy workshops: Multiday programs for specific employee subgroups such as women, Hispanics, African-Americans, and so on. These programs are designed to help participants better understand the dynamics of the organization culture and, thereby, manage those dynamics and their own careers more successfully. Programs also encourage informal networking among participants.

White male awareness workshops: Recently, some organizations have begun offering one-day programs to address the specific issues and concerns of white men. When they are well designed and facilitated, these programs go beyond mere "venting" and resemble efficacy workshops. They help participants understand how the organization culture is changing and what they must now do to effectively manage their own careers and succeed in the new environment.

High-impact awareness workshops: Unlike other categories already discussed, these programs are always multiday events. They are usually residential and delve deeper into the issues and underlying biases that often impede people's ability to interact effectively with *others* and value diversity.

Dialogue groups and core groups: Although facilitation techniques differ in each, both dialogue and core groups are prolonged, in-depth learning experiences. In each case, an intact, diverse small group of 6 to 12 employees meet periodically (weekly to monthly) to share and explore their core identities and deepen group understanding of how differences have shaped their perspectives and ability to interact with *others*. Dialogue groups are trained to use several specific techniques to explore complex diversity issues from many points of view: suspension of judgment, assumption identification, effective listening, open inquiry, and reflection. Core groups usually rely on a facilitator to help manage group interaction as well as to highlight and help the group analyze diversity issues.

Diversity conferences, issues seminars, video series, brown bags, and so on: In order to appeal to a wider population, many organizations also offer annual diversity conferences with multiple track programs for managers, diversity implementers, interested employees, and so on. Because one to two days off the job for awareness training is simply not a possibility for employees in many organizations, shorter seminars featuring guest speakers, videos, and facilitated discussion are also being designed as a more accessible alternative for exploring diversity issues and building personal awareness.

Business-Awareness Training

Although business-awareness training is frequently combined with personal-awareness training, the content and formats used are often distinctly different. Business-awareness training deals with the bottom-line reasons for adopting change. In most programs, emphasis is placed on changing workforce demographics and customer demographics. Expert presentations on the benefits that valuing diversity provides to both teams and organizations are usually included. To reach pragmatists, in-house presentations by influential change agents may also be part of a typical program. In addition, the costs of not valuing diversity that are identified in the organization's cultural assessment, such as lost sales and customer complaints, employee attrition, and so on, may be incorporated into business case histories for analysis and discussion.

Although some organizations host conferences to deal only with business diversity issues, many prefer to include a module or segment on the business case in their personal-awareness programs. These modules often include:

Senior leadership endorsements: Organizational leaders speaking about the linkages between valuing diversity, effective teamwork, innovative problem solving, and customer service.

Peer and expert testimonials: Specific, data-driven examples of how valuing diversity has led to enhanced teamwork, improved service, increased productivity, and so on.

Cultural assessment feedback summaries: Presentation and discussion of key issues/findings identified in organization climate assessments.

Legal issues and sexual harassment training: A discussion of the legal consequences of overt discrimination and sexual harassment. Case studies and discussion of the specific behaviors that do and do not constitute a violation of the law.

Diversity Skills Training

While diversity awareness training is aimed at enlarging participants' perspective about multicultural issues in the workplace, as well as their bottom-line impact, such programs are usually not designed to hone specific skills and modify behavior. In diversity skills training, the goals are quite different. Typically, participants are given a step-by-step framework for taking appropriate action. Once they understand the framework and the rationale behind it, they then practice using it. After each practice session, they are given peer feedback and then coached on how to perform the particular task more effectively. Depending upon the specific focus of training, this task may be:

- Mediating a cross-cultural conflict.
- Providing specific verbal feedback to *others*.
- Handling a harassment complaint.
- Listening and communicating more effectively with diverse employee groups.
- Interviewing diverse job applicants.

In contrast to awareness training, diversity skills training is designed to enhance or modify specific behavior. Through role plays, case study analysis, and simulations, participants put their frameworks for action into practice. They are coached and encouraged to refine their techniques and analytical abilities. At the end of training, they leave with a repertoire of new skills that can be transferred to real-world situations.

The following is a description of several types of diversity skills training that are becoming popular in many organizations:

Intercultural etiquette: These programs are often designed for employees with international business responsibilities. They detail many of the culture-specific habits and customs likely to be encountered when traveling and working within a specific country, as well as business etiquette requirements of particular importance. Participants leave training with a specific list of business and social do's and don'ts to help them interact more comfortably and successfully while on international assignments.

Intercultural communications: Programs in this category fall into two subgroups. The first group outlines patterns of interaction and assumption based upon country differences. These programs are often a more in-depth extension of the etiquette training just described. The second group of communications programs often focuses on interactive style differences. The origins of these stylistic differences are discussed in terms of core dimensions of diversity such as race, gender, and ethnicity.

Cross-cultural conflict resolution and mediation skills: As work teams become increasingly diverse, there is an increased need for impartial negotiators to help mediate diversity-related disputes between employees before these escalate into major intergroup conflicts. While not intended to replace the ombuds role in organizations, employee pairs who receive conflict-resolution training can be helpful in sorting out and resolving cross-cultural disputes between employees that, left unaddressed, can foster deep divisions between diverse groups in a work team and seriously damage cooperation and morale.

Cross-cultural coaching and performance feedback: These programs are often designed for managers who experience difficulty giving direct feedback to diverse employees. They may include values and style self-assessments as well as skill practice in assessing performance and delivering behavior-specific feedback.

Cross-cultural interviewing: Usually intended for hiring managers as opposed to dedicated employment interviewers, these programs help participants recognize the cultural filters that can interfere with objective data gathering and skills assessment.

Cross-cultural mentoring: Intended for managers with limited experience coaching and sponsoring *others,* these programs help individuals build stronger, more productive relationships by clarifying expectations between newly paired mentors and their protégées.

Group facilitation skills: These workshops are usually designed to prepare volunteers to deliver personal-awareness workshops. Content typically focuses on stand-up presentation skills, understanding the predictable dynamics of team diversity, personal and business awareness, and facilitation skill practice.

Appropriate Timing and Content

Both awareness and skill training are useful for employees in all segments on the Diversity Adoption Curve. However, *the appropriate timing of training as well as the breadth and depth of topics covered will vary greatly across the five groups.* For example, in the initial phase of implementation, there will be interest in personal-awareness training, but this interest will be concentrated among **innovators** and **change agents.** Among **pragmatists,** demand is likely to be greatest for business-awareness training in the form of change agent testimonials during this phase. In later phases of implementation, pragmatists are also likely to seek out specific skill-development training as particular problems arise with respect to managing diversity.

Among **skeptics** and **traditionalists,** early education should be limited to authority endorsements for the value of diversity from experts and organizational leaders. As change adoption spreads through other segments and becomes a majority endorsed effort, skeptics and traditionalists are likely to require diversity skills training in order to meet new job-performance standards. To the extent that their training is specific and behavior-based, they will be more likely to benefit from participation. However, because of their existing attitudes and predispositions towards this change, skeptics and traditionalists are unlikely to benefit from personal-awareness training. Not only will this be true during the initial phase of implementation, it is likely to remain so for several years thereafter.

Eventually, as mainstream support for valuing diversity solidifies, there may be increased pressure placed on skeptics and traditionalists to attend some personal-awareness training. However, unlike the other segments who benefit from group discussion and interaction, the personal-awareness needs of skeptics and traditionalists may be more effectively met through individual coaching and self-paced, multimedia education.

Currently, several consulting firms are working to develop the first CD/ROM diversity training title. When this product finally becomes available in the next year to two years, CD/ROM is likely to become a popular and more efficient method for delivering diversity awareness and skills training, particularly to skeptics and traditionalists. Because CD/ROM technology lends itself to confidential, self-paced learning and repetitive skill practice, it is an excellent tool for transferring knowledge, building specific competencies, and modifying behavior in a nonthreatening setting.

Leadership Training and Coaching

While organization leaders are as likely as any other group to represent each segment on the Diversity Adoption Curve, they seldom have the luxury of waiting years to begin supporting culture change. Their position in the institutional hierarchy demands that they understand and adopt change faster. What's more, because their strong endorsement of diversity carries great weight with skeptics and traditionalists, it is important that leaders stay somewhat ahead of the curve and move towards change adoption as rapidly as possible.

Because their opinions and actions influence a large percentage of employees in the organization, leaders need to be well informed about diversity issues as early in the implementation process as possible. It is also important for members of this group to be somewhat self-aware of biases and filters that can influence personal assumptions, expectations, and actions. To acquire information about the issues and build greater self-knowledge, leaders need education. Many also need follow-up coaching to assure that their actions do not inadvertently undermine the goals of the initiative.

In organizations where upward communication is heavily filtered, leaders lack direct access to candid feedback from employees about their personal impact. Because of glass-ceiling issues, many also have limited access to the candid opinions of *others* regarding the organization culture; yet effective diversity leadership requires increased knowledge about organizational issues, the concerns of *others*, and one's own biases and blindspots. Ongoing leadership training and coaching can help individuals acquire this knowledge.

While not a quick fix, ongoing leadership education can pay big dividends in increased executive understanding, comfort, and support for change throughout the implementation process.

Change Management Training

Finally, to assure that valuing diversity is positioned as a significant long-term culture change and not as an affirmative action program or quick fix, key implementers must become familiar with the principles of change management outlined in this book. With the help of the Diversity Adoption Curve, it is possible to implement diversity in a manner that minimizes resistance and maximizes acceptance. Rather than repeat the mistakes being made in some organizations, risk burnout themselves, or settle for less than full adoption, change implementers can now take reasonable steps to assure personal and organizational success. By becoming experts on adoption and the most effective methods for educating every segment, they can increase the likelihood that their organizations will succeed with valuing diversity where others have not.

The Segment Education Plan

The following chart outlines a comprehensive diversity curriculum that has been built to accommodate differences in readiness and need among all five segments on the Diversity Adoption Curve. It describes the types of education that are likely to be most appropriate for each segment during the initial and later stages of implementation.

While specific segment education is critical for adoption of change, this does not mean that valuing diversity should be isolated or excluded from generic training that is value-based. Instead, this value should also be referenced in all management and employee training that emphasizes organizational values and links these to appropriate behavior.

SEGMENT EDUCATION PLAN

Timing	Innovators	Change Agents	Pragmatists	Skeptics	Traditionalists
Phase I implementation (years 1 to 2)	Ongoing self-education Benchmarking of leading-edge organizations Personal-awareness training	Personal and business-awareness training Leadership skills and change management training Facilitator training	Business awareness: Change agent panels on "early success stories"	Ongoing leadership endorsements Legal requirements: EO, sexual harassment, ADA, etc.	Ongoing leadership endorsements Legal requirements: EO, sexual harassment, ADA, etc.
Phase II implementation (years 2 to 4)	Elective training: awareness and skill development Introduction to revised organization systems/ practices	Elective awareness and skills training Introduction to revised organization systems/ practices Follow-up facilitator training	Diversity skills training Introduction to revised organization systems/ practices	Diversity skills training Leader and expert panels on how diversity benefits the organization Continuous leadership endorsements Introduction to revised organization systems/ practices	Diversity skills training Continuous leadership endorsements Introduction to revised organization systems/ practices
Phase III implementation (years 4 to 7)	Elective dialogue/core group involvement	Elective high-impact awareness training Conflict resolution/ mediation training Elective dialogue/core group involvement	Elective awareness and skills training	CD/ROM awareness training Personal coaching Continuous leadership endorsements Diversity skills training	CD/ROM awareness training Personal coaching Continuous leadership endorsements Diversity skills training

A Flexible Curriculum

Instead of employing a single strategy to address the diverse training needs of all segments, an ideal diversity curriculum must be flexible. As we have discussed, a one-size-fits-all approach to educating the segments will simply not work. Instead, a comprehensive diversity curriculum should include appropriate core training for each segment and elective programs as well. Not only will the timing and introduction of core training differ for each segment, actual program content will differ as well.

The core programs should be competency-building programs. They should help each segment move closer to adoption through the acquisition of new awareness and new skills. Elective programs should encourage individuals within each segment to explore in greater depth particular aspects of diversity that are of interest to them. Like a well-honed college curriculum, the combination of core and elective education should equip individuals with both the general capabilities necessary for continued success and the additional understanding and insights required for personal satisfaction and growth.

> **Implementation Principle #14:**
>
> **Not only will the timing and introduction of core training differ for each segment, actual program content will differ as well.**

For some employees (innovators and change agents), the focus of diversity education should begin with personal awareness. For pragmatists, core training should focus on business awareness. For those skeptics and traditionalists with little interest in either of the above, it is important to focus core training on skill development. Which particular tools and skillsets will most skeptics and traditionalists require to interact more effectively with *others*? Which behaviors must be enhanced and/or modified to make them more successful? By mastering specific skill competencies in diversity training, skeptics and traditionalists are then more likely to begin building the confidence and comfort that are also required to adopt change. As such, core training should help these segments learn how to "act the part." Once this is accomplished, positive feelings about valuing diversity will then be more likely to follow.

SIXTEEN

Best Practices Across Organizations

lthough the valuing diversity movement is just getting started across most U.S. industries, some institutions have been engaged in implementing this culture change for several years. While we have already discussed several of the classic missteps made in many organizations when diversity is implemented, we have yet to examine the most effective implementation practices that are coming into wider use today. This chapter will discuss the best practices common to many organizations where early efforts to promote culture change and value diversity seem to be taking hold and showing signs of success.

Common Operating Assumptions

Before strategies are developed or tactical plans designed, organizations interested in diversity must make a fundamental decision. They must decide if the fundamental goal of their initiative is *greater diversity per se* or the creation of *a culture that values diversity.* In cases where companies choose the latter, one usually finds two operating assumptions at work. They are:

1. Valuing diversity is a new management paradigm. To institutionalize this change, the organization must be willing to rethink and revise certain basic assumptions, systems, and practices.

2. Successful diversity initiatives demand broad institutional involvement and support. As such, they can not succeed as HR programs.

At the root of the best practices described in this chapter, one typically finds these two assumptions that help inform both planning and decision making. These key assumptions influence the actions of organization leaders, managers, and change implementers. As such, they are important foundation blocks for all implementation activities.

Best Practices

In addition to having these underlying assumptions in common, organizations adopting the paradigm of valuing diversity are also employing several common practices in order to reach this goal. These best practices help accelerate adoption of change. By enhancing efficiency, increasing clarity, and reducing the potential for major missteps, they increase the probability that valuing diversity will succeed.

Although no organization has yet achieved full adoption of the value of diversity, some institutions engaged in diversity implementation are reporting encouraging signs of early progress. In an analysis of these implementation efforts, 10 specific practices appear to be common to many. When used concurrently and applied consistently, these practices are credited with enhancing implementation and leading to greater adoption across employee segments. *As best practices, they also share certain characteristics.* In particular, they help:

- Support the long-term goal of culture change.
- Position valuing diversity as a business strategy.
- Emphasize inclusion, mutual respect, and cooperation.
- Encourage innovation and empowerment.

The following is a description of the 10 most prevalent best practices employed in more successful implementation efforts today. *While comprehensive implementation efforts must go beyond these practices to successfully prepare the organization for change,* these 10 practices add value to implementation efforts and, together, help to accelerate adoption of change.

Practice #1: Setting the Context for Change

In more successful diversity initiatives, clearly positioning the intent and scope of the overall change effort is seen as a crucial first step.

To minimize confusion as well as build understanding and wide-spread support, a rationale for adopting change must be provided. When done effectively, context setting begins to answer several important questions about the what, how, and why of change.

In particular, early communications to set the stage for implementation should:

- Link valuing diversity to key business goals and changing customer demographics.

- Link valuing diversity to changing workforce demographics.

- Clarify the complementary intent of organizational EO/ AA and valuing diversity efforts.

Practice #2: Providing Ongoing Communication

As with any important new idea, valuing diversity requires corporate attention and public endorsement to gain recognition and wide-spread support among employees; therefore, in more successful change efforts, ongoing communication is viewed as an essential part of each phase of implementation.

Typically, both formal communication vehicles (e.g., newsletters, executive speeches) and informal vehicles are employed to help set the tone and get the word out. In some communications, authority endorsements and change agent testimonials are emphasized in order to build support within particular segments. In others, baseline themes that define and reinforce the business case for adopting change are emphasized.

Throughout implementation, core leadership team members manage communications as an integral part of the change process. As such, they make maximum use of all available vehicles to introduce the new paradigm and inform the entire organization of the coming change. Rather than rely on the organizational grapevine to spread the word, these core teams proactively shape key messages and manage information flow. Throughout implementation the goal of ongoing communication remains: using all available communication vehicles for ongoing reinforcement of organizational commitment to the value of diversity.

Practice #3: Developing Knowledgeable and Committed Leaders

Regardless of how strong grassroots support for valuing diversity may be in an organization, leadership support is even more crucial for successful culture change. Without this, implementation efforts are doomed to superficiality—unable to move beyond the awareness training stage to address systemic issues and create substantive change.

In virtually every successful implementation effort, leadership involvement is seen as crucial to long-term success; therefore, early identification and development of change agents in visible leadership roles is an important step in the overall process. In particular, more successful efforts are committed to:

- Encouraging enthusiastic, visible sponsorship at senior executive levels.

- Providing ongoing executive coaching and education.

Practice #4: Focusing on Data-Driven Change

Without data from many credible sources to highlight key issues and support planning decisions, each step in the implementation process can be viewed by some employees as "suspect." With the help of current and credible information about employee and customer demographics as well as organization climate and practices, it is easier to make the case for valuing diversity, set priorities, and manage change. What's more, all corporate activities to accelerate adoption are more readily understood by employees.

In successful implementation efforts, all actions to value diversity are data-driven. As a result, modifications to benefits, to human resources policies and practices, to performance-evaluation systems as well as to marketing and customer service programs are made based on the results of ongoing quantitative and qualitative assessments. All awareness and skills training development are also data-driven.

Within more successful implementation efforts, data collection is frequently used to help underscore the:

- Actual and potential benefits of leveraging diversity in the marketplace.

- Impact of the corporate culture/environment on diverse employee groups.
- Gaps in current employee profile data and glass-ceiling issues.

Practice #5: Providing Awareness and Skill-Based Training

In more successful organizations, the path to multicultural under-standing begins with awareness education, but does not end there. To put awareness into action, managers and employees must also hone specific skills and develop the interpersonal tools required for effective intercultural communication, conflict resolution, coaching, cooperative teamwork, and so on. Therefore, more effective diversity curricula balance awareness development and skill development. In addition, the resources of employee affinity groups are tapped to provide cultural enrichment and culture-specific education as a supplement to formal corporate training.

Rather than rely on a single educational approach to meet diverse needs, more successful organizations are beginning to recognize diverse segment education needs. As such they are becoming more committed to:

- Providing basic/advanced awareness education and how-to skills training as appropriate.
- Tapping employee affinity groups for diverse input and enrichment experiences beyond formal training.

Practice #6: Encouraging Ongoing Learning

While important learnings about cultural diversity often occur in formal training sessions, opportunities for new insight and growth do not end there; in fact, they are often greater in the day-to-day work environment. When work teams and individuals are encour-aged to take time on the job for dialogue and exploration of cross-cultural perspectives, continuous learning and team building can result. Therefore, in more successful implementation efforts, ongoing inquiry and awareness building are encouraged and viewed as a necessary part of culture change. These organizations supplement formal education and maximize employee learning by: fostering an open and supportive atmosphere in the workplace for inquiry, discussion, dialogue and productive conflict resolution.

Practice #7: Multicultural Mentoring

As more successful organizations work to increase diverse representation at every level, many have come to rely on mentoring programs to increase visibility and access to development opportunities among diverse, high-potential employees. The most successful of these programs are based on two key assumptions:

- Mentoring must be inclusive, not exclusive.

- Cross-cultural mentoring is a learning opportunity for protégés *and* for mentors.

In organizations that employ this best practice, innovator and change agent executives are routinely involved in mentoring projects. As learners themselves, they are coached and trained to serve as informal advisors for employees from diverse backgrounds.

Some successful mentoring programs are designed to be skip-level efforts. Some require executives to mentor *others,* as well as people of similar core identities. As they support the development of people who are similar to and different from themselves, these executive mentors continue to learn more about multicultural issues in their own organizations and effective ways to develop diverse resources.

Practice #8: Providing Flexible Benefits/Scheduling

Alignment of organizational benefit plans to support diversity in lifestyle, life stage, and individual need is another practice gaining support in more successful implementation efforts. As organizations affirm their commitment to diversity, some are acknowledging the need for more flexibility, fairness, and support in their employee benefit programs. In order to increase parity and create a culture that supports greater employee diversity, partner benefits, dependent care, wellness and work/life balance initiatives are now becoming an integral part of serious implementation efforts.

Unlike organizations that view benefits and work/family balance issues as "not relevant" or "off limits" in discussions of valuing diversity, organizations committed to this paradigm recognize the importance of aligning what they say about diversity and what they actually support through their employee benefit programs. Where there is a "disconnect" between the two, there is growing commitment in these organizations to closing the gaps that still exist between words and actions.

The overall goal of such gap closing efforts is to create and maintain an organizational environment where employees are highly effective and productive without sacrificing their personal and family quality of life. To achieve this result, more organizations are becoming committed to:

- Modifying benefits menus to more fully meet diverse employee needs.

- Assisting employees with work/family balance issues.

Practice #9: Linking Rewards to Effective Diversity Management

As with any business initiative, measurable results and metrics are key ingredients in effective diversity implementation efforts. In organizations committed to this new paradigm, results are now being tied more directly to manager compensation so that leaders and managers who value diversity benefit from proactive efforts.

So far, this approach has focused on using the carrot to encourage effective leadership and management among innovators and change agents, rather than on using the stick to discourage inappropriate behavior. Until valuing diversity is adopted by the majority, this strategy is a more effective way of highlighting success stories and encouraging others (pragmatists) to join up. However, as adoption increases, other methods of reward and punishment will also certainly be needed to institutionalize this change across all segments.

Given the early stage of implementation efforts in most companies, it is appropriate that current efforts focus on:

- Recognizing and publicizing effective diversity leadership efforts.

- Linking rewards to diversity management results.

Practice #10: Building Common Ground

In most organizations, early implementation efforts tend to highlight differences in access, inclusion, rewards, and recognition that exist within the corporate environment. While it is critical that these issues be recognized and addressed, more successful organizations also recognize the importance of building cross-cultural support and cooperation during each phase of change. Hence, in these organizations, dual emphasis is placed on understanding the differential impact of policies and practices on diverse groups *as well as* understanding commonalties in interest and need shared across all groups.

To help build cross-cultural understanding and support, more successful organizations look for innovative and meaningful ways to involve diverse employees in the implementation process. In some cases, they do this by creating a volunteer corps of facilitators and mediators who help disseminate information and, like good will ambassadors, share their enthusiasm for the new paradigm. In others, they create meaningful dialogue with employee affinity groups to better understand the issues from many perspectives and to encourage cooperation and mutuality across diverse groups.

Among more successful companies, building common ground includes:

- Communicating organizational commitment and strategy to all employees and customers.
- Creating a multicultural ambassador corps to build grassroots support.

As we have discussed throughout this book, diversity implementation is complex. To succeed, a comprehensive, long-term systems approach to change is required. While the 10 practices described in this chapter *can not* produce sustained culture change on their own, they *can* act as enablers of productive change and do appear to support adoption when they are used consistently.

Because successful experience with implementation is still rather limited, there are only 10 practices on the current list. In the future, as more organizations approach implementation with a change management focus and recognize segment differences, many more best practices will undoubtedly emerge. Until that time, it will be up to committed managers and implementers of diversity to develop new practices that accelerate change and, thereby, chart the yet-to-be-discovered path to full adoption.

SEVENTEEN

Towards Full Adoption

Today, we live in a society that is undergoing vast changes. Many of these societal changes are unprecedented in their scope. They impact every aspect of contemporary life and influence the fundamental ways in which we view ourselves, our future, and the world around us. Valuing diversity is one of these fundamental changes. But unlike some others that could move our society towards a less stable and productive future, this new paradigm offers enormous, positive potential and opportunity for renewal.

To capitalize on our diversity and create an inclusive, cooperative, and respectful workplace, leadership is now required; hence, for innovators and change agents, this book is a call to action. Rather than wait another day or even another hour, those committed to seeing the promise of diversity fulfilled must act without delay. They must work with renewed commitment to build bridges between diverse communities, encourage greater cooperation, mutual respect, and assure that there is a place at the table for everyone in their organizations.

Need for Wholistic Advocacy

To build cultures that value inclusion, cooperation, and mutual respect, implementers of diversity must do what has not been done before. They must become wholistic supporters of the new paradigm and advocate without impunity. As such, effective implementers must have as much empathy and understanding for the issues and concerns of *others* as they do for those affecting groups to which they belong. They must recognize the interdependent nature of this change and understand that *we will either win together or else all lose*. As such, their actions must be consistent with the stated value of diversity—inclusive rather than exclusive, respectful rather than disrespectful, trusting rather than suspicious, and, above all, cooperative rather than competitive.

Encouraging Broad Ownership

Because the value and power of diversity are contained in the experiences and perspectives of diverse people, managers and implementers must also assure that many voices are represented in the dialogue that precedes and accompanies meaningful culture change. As the change process unfolds, all diverse constituencies in an organization must be actively represented in key decision making. While this may lead to prolonged debate and discussion at times, it is essential that implementers be patient and remain committed to this process. For it is the new insights that result from such open dialogue that will lead to meaningful and lasting change.

This does not mean that conflicting goals and demands should be ignored or remain unresolved. To move forward, key implementers must be prepared to take action. However, sufficient time must first be devoted to hearing about and understanding the issues associated with culture change from many perspectives. As a result, the vision that emerges from these discussions will be more likely to accommodate and include greater diversity and, therefore, be supported across many core constituencies.

Diversity = Multidimensional Focus

To build broad support for change throughout the implementation process, diversity itself must be viewed through a wide-angle lens. Rather than focus on one or two core dimensions only, efforts to value diversity should take all primary dimensions into account. In addition, secondary dimensions of diversity should also be given attention when changes in organizational assumptions, expectations, policies, and practices are considered.

By acknowledging many dimensions of diversity that make a difference in individuals' lives, organizations set the stage for meaningful dialogue with employees about the ways in which the existing culture supports and delimits them and, as a result, their effectiveness. In addition, by defining diversity in a broad and inclusive way, every core constituency is guaranteed a place at the discussion table. When there is room at the table for all points of view, there is a higher probability that informed decision making and broad, lasting commitment to change will result.

Alignment with Business Strategies

Rather than separate diversity implementation from strategic business goals, it is more powerful, practical, and productive to align the two and, thus, build greater understanding and support for change. Although some segments of the organization (innovators and change agents) will be motivated to adopt change for social and personal reasons, the majority of employees will only be inclined to get on board with the new paradigm after they see a strong business connection and understand the impact that this change will have on their personal careers.

As implementers develop communications, training, and involvement programs to reach all five segments, they must continuously emphasize both the personal and strategic business benefits of adopting the value of diversity. If they fail to do so, they will literally preclude the possibility of successful adoption of this important change. In addition, as implementation proceeds, the value of diversity must evolve from a stand-alone initiative to become an integral part of the way business is done. As such, it should eventually be integrated into all strategic planning efforts and be treated as an integral part of key decisions that impact the bottom line. Until this is done, valuing diversity will not be fully institutionalized and, thus, will not be fully adopted.

Freedom to Pilot and Experiment

Because the path to successful adoption is just beginning to be explored, it is likely that some unknowns still lie ahead. Before any organization successfully completes the journey, additional piloting and testing of creative implementation strategies will be required. While new, innovative practices should be based on what is already known about diversity implementation, they must go beyond where organizations have gone before.

For example, while some institutions recognize the need for a segmented approach to implementation, none has fully utilized the Diversity Adoption Curve to design and implement this change. It is now time to do so.

Rather than restrict implementation efforts to the best practices that have proven to be moderately successful to date, committed organizations must encourage implementers to be innovative and risk-taking. This does not mean they should have license to be reckless. It simply means that diversity implementation must become more segmented and experimental as opposed to one-size-fits-all. Instead of benchmarking and reinventing a status quo approach that will not produce substantive change, diversity implementers need the skills, insights, and, at times, the counsel of professional consultants required to customize implementation for the particular needs of their organizations and the diverse needs of each segment.

Need for Passion, Compassion, and Forgiveness

Finally, after segment differences are factored into the plan, there remains a need for passion, compassion, and forgiveness in implementing this fundamental change. To remain effective and avoid burnout, implementers of diversity must build a personal and professional network that includes many innovators and change agents. Only then will they be able to maintain a deep, abiding passion for promoting this change.

In addition, as they reach out to pragmatists, skeptics, and traditionalists, implementers of diversity must find the compassion required to understand and empathize with these segments and the generosity of spirit required to forgive those who may appear openly hostile towards this change. Rather than move against their negative energy, we must learn to redirect it towards more productive, positive outcomes.

Today, in the workplace and throughout society, we have entered a new and exciting millennium—the millennium of diversity. Unlike the past, when the "golden rule" was used as a benchmark for effective human interaction, the new era of diversity demands more from each of us. Instead of "doing unto others as you would have them do unto you," we must now develop the understanding and empathy required to truly *know others*. With this greater knowledge, we can then "treat others as they would have us treat them."

To the extent that we are able to embrace this new golden rule, we can increase our own effectiveness as implementers of change. And as we help organizations understand and accept this new guiding principle as well, we can take satisfaction in knowing that full adoption of the value of diversity is at last becoming inevitable.

APPENDIX A

Valuing Diversity Implementation Checklist

The following is a checklist of actions described in this book and required to successfully implement diversity in an organization. As you read through the list, mark any items that have yet to be fully addressed in your organization and, therefore, will require further attention.

Start-Up Actions:

☐ Identify experienced external consulting resources.

☐ Select a core leadership team.

☐ Provide initial training for the core leadership team.

☐ Compile a complete business case for the value of diversity.

☐ Conduct a cultural assessment.

☐ Identify global diversity implementation issues.

☐ Create an overall implementation plan.

☐ Segment organization leaders.

☐ Involve change agent leaders.

☐ Develop a corporate diversity vision.

☐ Develop an initial communication plan and key start-up messages.

☐ Identify change agents at all organizational levels.

☐ Develop base-line communications for all segments regarding the business case for diversity.

Phase I Actions:

☐ Continue base-line business case communications to all segments.

☐ Review cultural assessment findings with all organizational leaders.

- ☐ Benchmark the best practices in innovative organizations.
- ☐ Provide diversity leadership training amd individual follow-up coaching.
- ☐ Provide core personal- and business-awareness training for change agents.
- ☐ Develop and communicate change agent success stories to pragmatists.
- ☐ Provide leadership endorsements and core business-awareness training in legal issues for skeptics and traditionalists.
- ☐ Begin aligning all HR systems (for recruitment, hiring, performance management, employee development, succession planning, benefits, etc.) with the value of diversity.
- ☐ Begin addressing gaps in current versus desired employee profile.
- ☐ Begin addressing glass-ceiling issues.
- ☐ Integrate the value of diversity in strategic business plans.

Phase II Actions:

- ☐ Continue base-line communications and specific segment communications.
- ☐ Introduce revised organization systems and practices to all segments.
- ☐ Continue aligning HR systems with the value of diversity.
- ☐ Continue addressing gaps in current versus desired employee profile.
- ☐ Continue addressing glass-ceiling issues.
- ☐ Continue providing leadership endorsements to all segments.
- ☐ Develop recognition and reward mechanisms for effective diversity leadership and management.
- ☐ Align affinity group goals and corporate valuing diversity goals.
- ☐ Create an ongoing interface between affinity groups and the core leadership team.

- ☐ Provide elective personal-awareness training for innovators and change agents.
- ☐ Incorporate value of diversity modules in all values-based management and employee training.
- ☐ Provide facilitator training for change agents.
- ☐ Involve change agents in training roll-out.
- ☐ Provide core business-awareness training for pragmatists.
- ☐ Provide core skills training for pragmatists, skeptics, and traditionalists.
- ☐ Tap affinity group resources for cultural enrichment education.
- ☐ Develop formal/informal mentoring initiatives.
- ☐ Measure the degree of change adoption in an annual employee opinion survey.
- ☐ Develop and implement a diversity management upward feedback process for managers and leaders.

Phase III Actions:

- ☐ Continue base-line communications and specific segment communications.
- ☐ Continue providing leadership endorsements to all segments.
- ☐ Introduce new/revised organization systems and practices to all segments.
- ☐ Complete the alignment of HR systems with the value of diversity.
- ☐ Close remaining gaps in current versus desired employee profile.
- ☐ Eliminate remaining glass ceilings.
- ☐ Expand recognition and reward systems to address gaps in the current versus desired employee and manager behaviors related to valuing diversity.
- ☐ Continue measuring degree of change adoption in an annual employee opinion survey.
- ☐ Utilize the diversity management upward feedback process for managers and leaders.

- ☐ Introduce advanced elective training: dialogue, high-impact workshops, core groups, and so on.
- ☐ Provide elective training to innovators, change agents and pragmatists.
- ☐ Provide core personal-awareness training to skeptics and traditionalists (CD/ROM).
- ☐ Provide personal coaching to skeptics and traditionalists.
- ☐ Provide conflict resolution training to change agents.
- ☐ Provide core skills training to skeptics and traditionalists.

NOTES

Chapter 2

1. Marilyn Loden and July B. Rosener, *Workforce America!: Managing Employee Diversity as a Vital Resource* (Homewood, IL: Irwin Professional Publishing, 1991), pp. 18–20.

Chapter 3

1. "'Glass Ceiling' Firmly In Place, U.S. Study Finds," *San Francisco Chronicle,* March 16, 1995, p. 1.

Chapter 5

1. Everett M. Rogers with F. Floyd Shoemaker, *Communication of Innovations: A Cross-Cultural Approach* (New York: The Free Press, 1971), pp. 182–5.

Chapter 6

1. Reginald A. Bowes, Unpublished Communications Papers, © 1980–1995. All rights reserved.

2. C. David Mortensen, *Communication: The Study of Human Interaction* (New York: McGraw Hill, 1972), pp. 101–4.

Chapter 9

1. "Diversity's Learning Curve: Multicultural Training's Challenges Include Undoing Its Own Mistakes," *The Washington Post,* February 5, 1995, Section H, p. 4.

Chapter 10

1. Howard Kohn, "Service with a Sneer," *New York Times Magazine,* November 6, 1994, p. 43.

2. Thomas McCarroll, "It's a Mass Market No More," *Time,* Fall 1993, p. 80.

Chapter 11

1. Michael Mobley and Tamara Payne, "Backlash! The Challenge to Diversity Training," *Training & Development,* December, 1992, p. 46.

2. Patricia Devine, Margo J. Monteith, and Julia Zuwerink, "Self-Directed versus Other-Directed Effect as a Consequence of Prejudice-Related Discrepancies," *Journal of Personality and Social Psychology,* 1993, Vol. 64, No. 2, pp. 198–210.

INDEX